A Chorus of Voices for
The Unchanging Heart of the Priesthood

"In refreshing contrast to recent trends which seek to redefine the Catholic priesthood and to lessen its evangelical demands, Father Thomas Acklin, O.S.B., proposes a solution to the present-day crisis which is both traditional and radical: entrance into the unchanging heart of Christ.

Father Acklin's analysis of present-day challenges to authentic priestly life and ministry is based on solid scriptural and Christian anthropological foundations, and is reflective of the great insights of Pope John Paul II. A true understanding and appreciation of the unchanging heart of the priesthood as a manifestation of the self-giving life and ministry of Christ the Servant and Priest will attract priestly vocations, help priestly renewal, and ultimately invigorate the Church."

BISHOP KEVIN C. RHOADES
Harrisburg, PA

"Father Acklin offers a positive, upbeat evaluation of current trends among seminarians and young priests. It is especially encouraging to discover that they do not have the hang-ups of the '70s and '80s and are seriously interested in prayer, self-denial, and the proven forms of asceticism that lead to personal holiness.

In a time when many Catholics have a false understanding of the priesthood—perhaps due to the influence of materialistic psychology, sociology, and secularism—this book refutes modern misconceptions and offers wise guidance for young men who want to dedicate their lives as priests of Jesus. . . . I recommend *The Unchanging Heart of the Priesthood* for priests of all ages, but especially for seminarians and young priests who are seeking good spiritual guidance and encouragement.

FR. KENNETH BAKER, SJ
Editor, *Homiletic and Pastoral Review*

"While wading into some contentious water, Father Acklin makes his own statement—clear and solid—about ordained, ministerial priesthood. Any change in the face of the priesthood, however responsive it may seem to contemporary challenges, must be legitimated by a rooting in a clear appreciation of the unchanging heart of the priesthood. His professional background—theological, spiritual, and psychological—brings a nuance, a realistic sensitivity, and a profound faith to his discussion of topics like human sexuality, intimacy, and celibacy for the priest—a balanced perspective often not seated at the table of such discussion."

Fr. George Aschenbrenner, SJ
Co-founder, Institute for Priestly Formation, Creighton University
Author of *Quickening the Fire in Our Midst:*
The Challenge of Diocesan Priestly Spirituality

"This book will be immensely helpful to anyone trying to contextualize the recent abuse scandals within the Church, while at the same time holding a profound love and reverence for the priesthood. Seminarians will find it particularly helpful and fruitful for spiritual reading. I heartily recommend it."

Msgr. Steven P. Rohlfs, STD
Rector, Mount St. Mary's Seminary

"This book is much-needed surgery. Like a good surgeon, Father Acklin is unflinching, realistic, demanding, and meticulous, yet always respectful and constructive, with healing as his goal. Catholics need this book, for a full understanding—and then a full flourishing—of Catholicism in America."

Mike Aquilina
Vice President, St. Paul Center for Biblical Theology

The
UNCHANGING
HEART
of the
PRIESTHOOD

The
UNCHANGING
HEART
of the
PRIESTHOOD

A Faith Perspective on the Mystery and the
Reality of Priesthood in the Church

FR. THOMAS ACKLIN, O.S.B.

Foreword by Bishop Donald W. Wuerl
Preface by Fr. Benedict Groeschel, C.F.R.

EMMAUS
ROAD
PUBLISHING

Steubenville, Ohio
A Division of Catholics United for the Faith

Emmaus Road Publishing
827 North Fourth Street
Steubenville, OH 43952

Library of Congress Control Number: 2005925600
ISBN: 1-931018-29-4
ISBN: 978-1-931018-29-6

Cover design and layout by
Beth Hart

On the Cover:
Christ by Leon Bannat
Réunion des Musées Nationaux / Art Resource, NY
and
Italy Mourns Death of Pope John Paul II
ZUMA Press / NewsCom

I will give you shepherds after my own heart.
—Jeremiah 3:15

Contents

Foreword

*T*he mystery and wonder of the priesthood is intimately tied into an all-embracing mystery that we call "the Church." To understand one implies a grasp of the other. In his most recent book, *The Unchanging Heart of the Priesthood: A Faith Perspective on the Reality and the Mystery of Priesthood in the Church*, Father Thomas Acklin, O.S.B., invites us to consider both, and he does so with theological insight and pastoral experience.

At the installation of every pastor, I take the opportunity to contextualize his priestly ministry in the wider reality of the Church. Only then can we begin to recognize what an extraordinary ministry Christ has left us in the priesthood. Pastor and flock, leader and faith community, spiritual father and God's family—these are all correlative terms because they are mutually complementary realities.

Jesus Christ, the Word and the Son of God whom the Father sent into the world, proclaimed the Good News of reconciliation between God and His children. His preaching, confirmed by signs and wonders, reached its summit in the Paschal Mystery, the supreme word of the divine love with which the Father spoke to us. On the Cross, Jesus showed Himself, to the greatest possible extent, to be the Good Shepherd who lays down His life for His sheep. Exercising the supreme and unique priesthood by the offering of Himself, Christ surpassed the ritual priesthood and sacrificial offerings of the Old Testament by fulfilling them. He bore the sins of us all on the Cross. Rising from the dead and being made Lord, He reconciled us to God and laid the foundation for the people of the New Covenant, which is His Church.

Christ is the image of God, breaking into our world to announce that to believe is to walk in the light. To walk in the light is to live in the kingdom. To live in the kingdom is to build up that kingdom, which in its fullness is God's new creation. There are clear and multiple implications to this understanding of the nature of the Church and priestly ministry.

At the heart of our Catholic faith is the understanding that Christ continues to be with us in and through His Church. Christ is really and truly present to us in His risen, glorified body through every sacrament we celebrate and when we unite ourselves in prayer. The proclamation of the kingdom of God in our midst is the declaration that salvation comes to us through our participation in the life of the Church and through the unfolding of the Paschal Mystery in sacramental experience that makes us one with Jesus. The Church is not incidental to salvation. It is the way to our redemption.

What is true of the Church is true of priesthood. Holy Orders is the sacrament by which the mystery of God, present with us in His Church, is structured and ordered in a visible, tangible human way, so that the invisible divine gift might invest all of us. Priests minister both in the name and in the person of Christ.

Consequences follow on the revelation that Christ is the eternal High Priest, who shares His ministry with those called and anointed by the Spirit in Holy Orders. Some of the mystery of priesthood and a part of its implications for the life of the Church have been downplayed or ignored (and in some cases even denied) in some of the literature on the Catholic priesthood today. While it was far more fashionable in the sixties and seventies to present what was called a "low ecclesiology," and therefore a diminished vision of priesthood, there is still a lingering residue of that type of writing available today.

Because of the moral lapse of a number of priests in this country, and because of the extraordinary attention directed to this tragedy, we are all witnessing a public reevaluation of the nature and value of Catholic priesthood. This assessment is taking place in the media, some of which are hostile to Gospel values and, in particular, to the consistent pro-life proclamation by the Catholic

Church. It is not surprising then that the assessment is negative and the expression of it often hostile.

Editorials in several national news magazines have called for the ordination of women, the abandonment of the more than millennium-old tradition of a celibate priesthood, and, in some instances, the rejection of the Church herself as a means of salvation. Radio and television talk shows and their guests have also used this tragedy as a vehicle to bring forward countless other unrelated items of their own agenda. Through all this we need to make our way, clarifying what is truly at issue and keeping a proper perspective.

Father Thomas Acklin addresses some of the questions raised in relation to the Church's teaching on the priest as the man configured to Christ, the Head of the Church. He also speaks to the question of priestly celibacy and to the claims by some that it has failed the Church and many priests. What Father Acklin brings to this study is a calm and reasoned presentation of the Church's teaching and a lucid analysis of the experience of celibate priesthood today, in contrast to those who challenge it.

In chapter 1, Father Acklin deals with what he calls "the changing face on the unchanging heart." Here, he guides us into a reflection on what the Church says of her priesthood. The author notes that even in a changing sociological context—with fewer priests, and therefore a refocusing on the specific ministry of the priest—there remains a core of teaching on the essence of priesthood that is unchanged over millennia. In addition to his theological studies, Father Acklin has degrees in and is a professional practitioner of psychology and psychoanalysis. Even a brief review of his biography assures us of his competence to deal with questions that others sometimes speak of anecdotally, without scientific support or precision.

When we turn to the next four chapters—2 through 5—we find Father Acklin bringing both his theological and psychological studies as well as his experience and expertise to bear on issues that, especially today, need to be treated with the high level of profes-

sionalism that he brings to the task. Thus, his discussion on power
and authority in the priesthood, sexuality in the priesthood, homosexuality in the priesthood, and celibacy and intimacy are not only
engaging but also informative and inspirational.

Perhaps nothing is more challenged (and challenging) in priesthood today than celibacy. Celibacy is an eschatological sign. By
transcending every contingent human value, the celibate priest
associates himself in a special way with Christ as the final and
absolute Good and shows the freedom of the children of God.
While the value of the sign and holiness of Christian marriage is
fully recognized, celibacy for the sake of the kingdom nevertheless
more clearly displays that spiritual fruitfulness or generative power
of the New Law, by which the apostle knows that, in Christ, he is
the father of his communities.

There does not seem to be any question that there is a profound sign value to the gift of celibacy. It bears witness to what
we hold in faith—to the world of the risen Lord. In terms of the
world of the Spirit—the kingdom of God—the fullness of love
is obviously a non-physical reality. To attempt to express that
otherworldly, spiritual love in this world of time, space, and physical limitation is an extraordinary venture—one that requires a
special gift from God.

Celibacy is a means to gain freedom from the limitation of our
own legitimate, human physical expressions. The freedom gained
through celibacy is a freedom to consecrate oneself, a freedom to
love in a way that is totally spiritual and so self-giving as to reflect
a fullness of love that will only be realized in the kingdom of God.
The value of celibacy is that it prepares, in proclamation and in
fact, for the fullness of the kingdom.

What I find particularly encouraging in Father Acklin's writing
is the recognition that while there are objections to celibacy, there
are also legitimate responses to those critiques. As a good teacher,
he offers us convincing, valid responses that ultimately help to
enrich the fuller vision of priesthood and Church as great gifts
from God.

The final chapter, "Priestly Spirituality and Renewal," can be seen as a meditation on living out priesthood today. This is good retreat material that speaks not so much to the theology of priesthood, but to the daily experience of it. Here Father Acklin, the priest-counselor and spiritual director, comes to the fore.

The Unchanging Heart of the Priesthood is a welcome addition to today's discussions on the priesthood and a valuable contribution to the effort to support and sustain the Church's vision of priesthood as it is experienced and lived by so many good priests, religious and secular, throughout this country.

MOST REV. DONALD W. WUERL
Bishop of Pittsburgh

Preface

*I*n the past three decades, the two-thousand-year-old institution of the Catholic priesthood, like most other things in the life of the Church, has undergone a good deal of change. Much of this change has been social and psychological, relating to how bishops and priests see themselves and actually fit into the life of the Christian community. The image of the somewhat distant monsignor with three assistants has given way to the very busy pastor on a very tight schedule, serving the needs of a large parish as best as he can alone. He relies on the laity, and they rely on him. These changes are hardly surprising, and are for the best. As a living thing the Church, together with the priesthood, has changed and adapted to a rapidly changing world. The factors contributing to this time of transition are to be found in things as diverse as the level of education, the shrinking of the globe by communication and commerce, and the study of history on a more secular basis. Changes come from things as good as the renewal of the Church called for by the Second Vatican Council, and from forces as negative as the so-called sexual revolution, the decline of family life, and a wave of theological confusion in which whole societies— some of them as large as Christian nations and some as compact as religious orders—appear to have lost their way.

At the time of the publication of this book, the Catholic Church in the United States has been rocked by the greatest crisis in its history. Although the severity of the crisis has been exaggerated by the secular media's frenzy against the Church, this hostile secular press has nonetheless done the Church a service by bringing out the effects of moral confusion and relativism that is sweeping through almost all religious denominations in the English-speaking world.

This crisis has revealed how much we as a Church need to return to our foundations, to our essential teachings and principles, and to our identity as the historical reality founded by Christ and entrusted by Him with His sacraments and teachings. Much of the confusion in the Church is focused on the priesthood; Father Thomas Acklin is literally in the right place and at the right time with answers to the questions heard on all sides.

A variety of writers, most of them ordained members of the Catholic priesthood, have addressed the roots of change, the need for further change, and what they see as the best way to accomplish this. Some of these writers have firmly held on to Catholic Tradition, rooted in the New Testament and in the tradition of the priesthood from the very first centuries of the Church. Preeminent among these was Pope John Paul II. His substantial writings on the priesthood focus on the life, identity, spirituality, and formation of priests. Other writers have also sought to restore the identity of the priesthood with its theological foundations but still have not hesitated to engage various contemporary trends that appear to be eroding the very foundation of this institution that is so essential to the life of the Church. These writers are both contemporary and traditional. Other writers, displaying a remarkable ignorance of or disregard for its theological and historical foundations, have failed to see the priesthood as actually founded by Christ or even as an essential element in the life of the Church that Christ founded. These writers have apparently confused the priesthood with the pastoral ministry that evolved in the Protestant churches when the sacramental character and the divine institution of the priesthood were denied. With scarcely a nod to history, they have done the equivalent of trying to grow figs from thistles. They have made all kinds of radical suggestions that, if followed, would bring any historically rooted institution to ruin.

Finally, there are those who have openly questioned the whole concept of the sacramental priesthood. With Hans Küng, they have asked, "Why have priests at all?" Cardinal Avery Dulles has described these writers, popular with some of the Catholic intelligentsia, as proposing a priesthood indistinguishable from congregational Protestantism, a model he was quite familiar with early on.[1]

The Catholic priesthood, along with religious life, has been buffeted by other forces at this same time. The uncritical use of popular theories in the behavioral sciences, especially clinical psychology, has proved to be as helpful as putting "new patches on old wineskins." And at the same time, a tendency in biblical studies that John Paul II called a "rationalist prejudice against the supernatural" has undermined the faith of many of the clergy. I know from three decades of my own work with priests that the skepticism about revelation and the denial of the transcendent have contributed significantly to the mass exodus of clergy from several denominations. The pursuit of Catholic spirituality, motivated by prayer, self-knowledge, and self-discipline, and expressed in generous good works, has been replaced by innumerable gimmicks aimed at self-fulfillment or self-realization. All this has led, as it must lead, to a loss of faith and even to a decline of Christian morality, resulting in most painful and debilitating scandals—especially the most recent one revealing the sexual abuse of minors.

In 2000, Father Donald Cozzens, then rector of a Catholic seminary, was prompted by his work with priests over three turbulent decades to attempt to assess the causes of decline in numbers and satisfaction of priests. His book *The Changing Face of the Priesthood* released a firestorm of disagreement, especially among younger clergy and seminarians. In my contacts with these younger men I found deep disagreement with Father Cozzens among this age group, and resentment at his assumption that there was a trend for them to be homosexual.

Father Cozzens' book drew an immediate critical response from several quarters. Bishop Earl Boyea, then rector of the Josephinum in Columbus, Ohio, a seminary under the jurisdiction of the Holy See, wrote a thoughtful critique especially emphasizing Father Cozzens' misreading of the situation. He contrasts his experience with Cozzens' and finds big differences in their impressions. This is very important because Father Cozzens admits that his opinions are based on impressions.[2]

In November 2000, I wrote a critique for *Inside the Vatican* in which I deplored the apparent lack of any moral judgment on Father Cozzens' part when describing immoral sexual behavior on the part of some of the clergy. I rejected his assessment of younger clergy as men who did not follow Christian teaching on chastity. I also expressed my opinion that his use of Freudian psychoanalytic concepts in relationship to the priest was contrived. But my strongest objection to *The Changing Face of the Priesthood* was the painful lack of any reference to the transcendental meaning of the mystery of Christ and His kingdom. Although Father Cozzens indicates that priests need an element of transcendence in their lives, his description of this essential spiritual element is totally naturalistic. While we all can catch a glimpse of the glory of God in a beautiful sunset, our most powerful and transcendent experience should be the mystery of Christ as our Redeemer and Savior, which we have during prayer and meditation. The daylight of this world is only a pale symbol of the eternal light that shines on us through Jesus Christ and the grace that He won for us on the Cross.

In one way, I'm grateful that Father Cozzens' book appeared. Without meaning to do so, he has revealed the reasons why vocational recruitment and seminary education have languished in recent decades. *The Changing Face of the Priesthood* is "exhibit A"—firsthand and incontrovertible evidence that the vocational crisis in the priesthood and religious life is caused at least partly, if not primarily, by a formation that has been seriously deficient. In many cases Catholic seminary training has been essentially naturalistic, theologically confused, subtly hostile to the teachings of the highest pastoral authority of the Church, and often spiritually deficient. I have been teaching in various seminaries for forty years, and I have the scars to prove it. Every person responsible for or interested in our recovery from the present vocational crisis ought to read *The Changing Face of the Priesthood* and then read some of the critiques. Without apparently meaning to do so, Father Cozzens has given a graphic illustration of the core problem, and I am grateful to see that he has elicited a powerful negative response from most seminarians and young priests.

All over the English-speaking world, there are seminarians and young priests concerned about the lack of Catholic and priestly identity in their training. Of course, there are plenty of exceptions to the poor performance of seminaries and religious training programs. Some seminaries as well as individual faculty members and formations have done a good job; but the truth is that there are sharp ideological divisions. These divisions are eliciting an intense desire on the part of seminarians and young priests for a more enthusiastic and integrated presentation of the Catholic faith, the Gospel, and the priestly identity. There are several very encouraging examples of seminaries that have been reformed, often with great personal effort on the part of the reformers. If we could hear from those who are no longer in the seminary but who would be if they had found a fervent commitment to Christ, we would realize how many desperately needed vocations have been lost in the past decades.

Enter now Father Thomas Acklin, O.S.B. Father Thomas has been rector of a successful seminary with an enthusiastic group of students. He has faced the same problems as rectors everywhere. With the strong support of his monastic superior, Archabbot Douglas Nowicki of Saint Vincent, he has tackled the same problems as every rector, which I have outlined above.

Here he gives us a solid, thoroughly thoughtful and psychological analysis of the present difficulties and brings this to a logical conclusion based on well-thought-out arguments. Often accurate and realistic analyses and solutions may not be as enjoyable to read as exposés and quick fixes; however, the pursuit of truth is an arduous and challenging experience. This is why it is worth the intellectual effort to search for truth. Father Thomas analyzes the evangelical, theological, and historical foundations of the priesthood. If you don't know and understand those, you should not agree to facile answers about how to change the priesthood. We have seen the catastrophic effect of this kind of "quick fix," superficial thinking on religious communities. If you don't understand psychoanalytic theory, its valid applications and its conclusions, you should not use it to put the priesthood on the couch, as Father Cozzens and others have done. Father Thomas has the background, professional training, and certification in psychoanalysis that very few priests have. Although I have my own reservations about how this theory can be applied to the priesthood, Father Thomas offers a very serious and professional critique of Father Cozzens' analysis.

A new round of debate on the priesthood is starting with the dreadful impetus supplied by the crisis of sexual misbehavior. It is a crucial round, since the number of priests and seminarians is in dramatic decline. Father Cozzens did a service by putting the debate out in the open, although I think he is clearly on the losing side. Father Thomas is, so far, the most articulate and informed voice to look thoroughly at the issues that Father Cozzens raised.

The Unchanging Heart of the Priesthood needs to be read carefully, in sections. It is not a bedside book. The author explores the whole theology of the priesthood, as well as its application in the present situation, and looks at the criticisms leveled at it by Father Cozzens and others. Father Acklin's strength in theology and in psychology and psychoanalysis is obvious.

If you are interested in the welfare of the Catholic Church and its priesthood, and if you wish to be seriously informed about the issues, I highly recommend this book. From a more inspirational point of view, you will find similar ideas practically applied to the priesthood in Archbishop Timothy Dolan's book *Priests for the Third Millennium.* The serious reader is probably already familiar with George Weigel's very insightful analysis of the scandal, *The Courage to Be Catholic*; and written for a more popular audience, my own attempt to discover a way out of the catastrophe, *From Scandal to Hope.*[3]

All of these works, and probably some others coming along, present a new statement of the authenticity of the Catholic priesthood as it has been traditionally known. Every priest should get on his knees and begin to look at his life from the viewpoint of these serious contributions to understanding his vocation. Every friend of the Church and every loyal Catholic should be doing the same thing.

FR. BENEDICT J. GROESCHEL, C.F.R.

Acknowledgments

Any priest who picks up this book may know that it is dedicated to him, and particularly to all the priests and seminarians with whom I have had the great privilege of sharing the priesthood and the powerful gift of our sacramental configuration with Christ. In particular, I would like to dedicate this work to Pope John Paul II, who served the third-longest pontificate in history, and who during this time so profoundly renewed the priesthood through his writing and by his example. I dedicate it as well to his able and humble successor, Pope Benedict XVI.

I would like to recognize some among so many who have nourished my vocation to the priesthood: in my childhood, my mother; Father Paul Holzer and so many Pittsburgh diocesan priests; Sister Rose Veronica and the Sisters of Saint Joseph of Baden, Pennsylvania; and my lifelong friend, Bishop David Zubik. I recognize my intimate companions during the time of my priesthood: my director for a quarter of a century, Father Silvan Rouse, CP; Sister Jeannette Plante, CSC; Sister Mary Ann Nunlist, CP; Father Justin Matro, O.S.B.; Father John Conway and Father Boniface Hicks, O.S.B. I express gratitude to all those who have supported me in my ministry as a priest: Archabbot Douglas Nowicki, O.S.B., and my monastic confreres at Saint Vincent Archabbey; my fellow servants and colleagues at Saint Vincent Seminary, and all those whom I have taught and served as rector; and my spiritual directees and counselees, by whom I have been taught so much. Finally, I am also deeply grateful to Mike Aquilina, Scott Hahn, Sue Answine, Carrie Cusick, and all those who encouraged me in this work.

About the Author

*F*ather Thomas Acklin, a Benedictine monk, first professed vows in 1976 at Saint Vincent Archabbey in Latrobe, Pennsylvania. He was ordained a priest in 1980 and studied theology and psychology of religion at the Catholic University of Louvain in Belgium, where he earned the STD (Doctor of Sacred Theology). He undertook psychoanalytic training at the Belgian School of Psychoanalysis and graduated from the Pittsburgh Psychoanalytic Institute. Father Acklin then served as master of junior-professed monks for four years and as president-rector of Saint Vincent Seminary for twelve years. He is a member of the Fellowship of Catholic Scholars, the Pittsburgh Psychoanalytic Society and Foundation, the American Psychoanalytic Association, and the International Psychoanalytic Association. He is certified in the psychoanalysis of adults by the International Board of Accreditation and Certification in Psychoanalysis and the National Association for the Advancement of Psychoanalysis. Currently, Father Acklin is professor of theology and psychology at Saint Vincent College and Saint Vincent Seminary, where he has taught since 1976, and is a faculty member of the Pittsburgh Psychoanalytic Institute and Foundation.

Abbreviations

Old Testament
Gen./Genesis
Ex./Exodus
Lev./Leviticus
Num./Numbers
Deut./Deuteronomy
Josh./Joshua
Judg./Judges
Ruth/Ruth
1 Sam./1 Samuel
2 Sam./2 Samuel
1 Kings/1 Kings
2 Kings/2 Kings
1 Chron./1 Chronicles
2 Chron./2 Chronicles
Ezra/Ezra
Neh./Nehemiah
Tob./Tobit
Jud./Judith
Esther/Esther
Job/Job
Ps./Psalms
Prov./Proverbs
Eccles./Ecclesiastes
Song/Song of Solomon
Wis./Wisdom
Sir./Sirach (Ecclesiasticus)
Is./Isaiah
Jer./Jeremiah

Lam./Lamentations
Bar./Baruch
Ezek./Ezekiel
Dan./Daniel
Hos./Hosea
Joel/Joel
Amos/Amos
Obad./Obadiah
Jon./Jonah
Mic./Micah
Nahum/Nahum
Hab./Habakkuk
Zeph./Zephaniah
Hag./Haggai
Zech./Zechariah
Mal./Malachi
1 Mac./1 Maccabees
2 Mac./2 Maccabees

New Testament
Mt./Matthew
Mk./Mark
Lk./Luke
Jn./John
Acts/Acts of the Apostles
Rom./Romans
1 Cor./1 Corinthians
2 Cor./2 Corinthians
Gal./Galatians

Eph./Ephesians
Phil./Philippians
Col./Colossians
1 Thess./1 Thessalonians
2 Thess./2 Thessalonians
1 Tim./1 Timothy
2 Tim./2 Timothy
Tit./Titus
Philem./Philemon
Heb./Hebrews
Jas./James
1 Pet./1 Peter
2 Pet./2 Peter
1 Jn./1 John
2 Jn./2 John
3 Jn./3 John
Jude/Jude
Rev./Revelation (Apocalypse)

Church Documents
All Church documents are available at www.vatican.va.

LG   Second Vatican Council, Dogmatic Constitution on the
      Church *Lumen Gentium* (November 21, 1964).

PDV   Pope John Paul II, Post-synodal Apostolic Exhortation
      on the Formation of Priests *Pastores Dabo Vobis*
      (March 25, 1992).

PO   Second Vatican Council, Decree on the Ministry and
      Life of Priests *Presbyterorum Ordinis* (December 7, 1965).

CHAPTER ONE

The UNCHANGING HEART *beneath the* CHANGING FACE

CRISIS OF SOUL

*T*he face of the Catholic priesthood is changing! Although this has always been the case, presently it may seem to us that the priesthood is perhaps changing more at this time than at any previous epoch in the history of the Church. If this is indeed a time of singular flux and change in the identity of the priest, and if it seems that these changes may be driven by crisis and scandal, it is all the more important for us to remember that behind the changing face of the priesthood remains the saving face of Jesus Christ,[1] who is the *unchanging heart* of the priesthood, and in terms of whom any change must be assessed.

As Jesuit Cardinal Avery Dulles notes in his excellent theological reflection *The Priestly Office*, new theological paradigms of priesthood have arisen, especially since the Second Vatican Council.[2] Father Hans Küng in his 1972 book *Why Priests?* could not seem to find a satisfactory answer to his own question. Observing, as Vatican II has reminded us, that all believers are priests, Küng states that the terms "priest" and "hierarchy" should be abolished: instead, "leaders" and "presiders" should administer the Eucharist and forgive sins. He further asserts that in the absence of these presiders anyone can administer the sacraments. Dominican

Father Edward Schillebeeckx agreed in his 1981 book *Ministry: Leadership in the Community of Jesus Christ*, in which he rejects any "ontological" understanding of the character of sacramental priesthood, concluding that any non-ordained believer could validly celebrate the Eucharist in an emergency.[3] The Vatican Congregation for the Doctrine of the Faith reacted critically to both of these theologians, though the influence of their thinking continues. Indeed, the question of whether there is even an adequate biblical foundation for the sacramental understanding of priesthood has been raised many times in the history of the Church, especially since the Protestant Reformation.

Even more serious than the challenge that has been raised concerning the nature of the priesthood is that concerning the state of those who are already ordained: the question of whether priests themselves are undergoing a crisis of soul. Serious questions have been raised about the sexual misconduct of priests and seminarians.[4] Scandal has swept through the Church over priests who do not live up to the promise of celibacy or who lead double lives in other ways, sometimes even engaging in criminal behavior such as pedophilia or other forms of sexual abuse or addiction.[5] Those who have worked many years in priestly formation have sometimes questioned the quality of candidates. They have voiced their concerns about what is really going on in priestly life, noting an underlying lack of sexual integration among the candidates and lamenting the poor preparation they have been given for a life of celibacy.[6]

My response in this book will likewise come from inside the priesthood—certainly from my own priestly life, which has been primarily dedicated to the ongoing formation of men for the priesthood. I propose first to consider the foundations for a theology of priesthood, and then to consider some of the issues raised by those who wonder whether there is a crisis in the priesthood. I will devote particular attention to celibacy, sexuality, and intimacy as these are lived out in the reality of priestly ministry in the present life of the Church.

THE THREE FUNCTIONS OF PRIESTHOOD

Cardinal Avery Dulles has entitled his book on the priesthood *The Priestly Office*. In what sense is priesthood an "office," and what are its functions? Let us immediately insist that the notion of priestly office can only draw meaning from Christ and His self-emptying love within His unconditional self-gift to the Father. Any theology of priesthood, ministry, office, or institution must be developed out of the *kenosis* (cf. Phil. 2:6) of Christ and lived out in the reality of the Church.[7]

Traditionally, the three functions of priesthood in the Church are the *prophetic*, the *priestly*, and the *royal*. How do these constitute a viable concept of ministerial priesthood, coherent with the Bible, Catholic Tradition, and the teaching of Vatican Council II? Can one individual perform all the facets of these three functions—ministry of the Word in its prophetic force, worship in its priestly dimensions, and shepherding in its pastoral engagement? Have terms like "royal" and "priestly," notions derived from the Letter to the Hebrews in reference to the unique priesthood of Jesus (10:14), outlived their meaningfulness? Moreover, how can charisms like prophecy be exercised within institutional structures? If these charisms were not restricted to ordained priests, might they not be more fully expressed by others? Has there been a tendency to focus all the power in one office, in a way that is patriarchal and unbiblical? And are there roots in the Old Testament for the way the Church understands priesthood and for the three priestly functions?

PRIESTHOOD IN THE NEW TESTAMENT
Old Testament Roots

In the Old Testament, the entire nation of Israel is described as a priestly people (Ex. 19:6). Yet alongside this priestly people there existed a consecrated priesthood, set apart and dedicated to sacred tasks such as offering sacrifice on behalf of all the people. These priests and Levites became the ones to take charge of the holy objects in the Temple (Ezra 8:28), and they alone are permitted to enter the most holy places (2 Chron. 23:6, 35:5). In this sense, two groups constituted Old Testament priesthood: the priestly people, and those with a more specialized priesthood. This second type of priesthood is primarily cultic and derives from a state of holiness; its functions include prophecy and governance over the people.[8]

Unlike Saint John the Baptist, whose father was a priest descended from the priestly tribe of Levi and whose mother descended from the priestly tribe of Aaron, Jesus was born into the tribe of Judah and not into hereditary priesthood.[9] Let us examine how the unique priesthood of Jesus came to be understood in the New Testament.

The Letter to the Hebrews

Priesthood in the New Testament moves beyond "the liturgical 'commemoration of sin'" (Heb. 10:3), which is "replaced by the memorial" of Jesus (Lk. 22:19; 1 Cor. 11:25), "since it makes present what is definitive and makes full satisfaction for sin."[10] The Letter to the Hebrews links the priesthood of Jesus Christ to the priesthood of Melchizedek (cf. Heb. 5:6–10, 6:20, 7:2, 17), who is at once priest, prophet, and king. A priest without ancestry or caste entitling him to the priesthood, like the Son of God, he is a priest forever (cf. Heb. 7:3). This offering of Melchizedek foreshadows the sacrifice of Christ, who is Himself the one Sacrifice, the one Mediator (cf. Heb. 9:15).

The high priesthood of Jesus is not one of self-exaltation, but is by God's appointment (cf. Heb. 5:5). Although He is God's Son, in the days of His flesh Jesus had to learn obedience through what He suffered, had to pray and shed tears, and thus become able to sympathize with human weakness (cf. Heb. 5:7–8). Tempted in every respect, "yet without sinning" (Heb. 4:15), Jesus "made purification for sins" and is now seated "at the right hand of the Majesty on high" (Heb. 1:3), "designated by God a high priest" (Heb. 5:10).

Thus the heavenly and eternal priesthood of Jesus Christ transcends the Levitical priesthood and the order of Aaron, being instead of the same order as Melchizedek. Jesus is eternal, suggesting His divine preexistence, yet He is also human, suggesting His Incarnation.[11] Jesus became human so that, taken from men like every high priest, He could "act on behalf of men in relation to God" (Heb. 5:1) and be able "to make expiation for the sins of the people" (Heb. 2:17). As high priest, He mediates a new covenant (Heb. 9:15), an eternal redemption ensured by the eternal Spirit as the fruit of His sacrifice (Heb. 9:14). Thus, "the priesthood of Christ had its beginning at the Incarnation but attained its full reality only at the moment in which he entered into heaven. . . . The heavenly Christ exercises his priesthood by interceding for mankind. . . . If the essential task of the priest is not only to offer sacrifice but to intercede on behalf of mankind, the fundamental intention of love appears more vividly in the priesthood."[12] The mediation of the human priest links the spatial and temporal situation of the people of God with God Himself—an access achieved through orientation to and in the act of Christ, not through the human celebrant.[13] The mediation of Christ the High Priest is linked with the sacrifice of the Shepherd by "the God of peace, who brought again from the dead our Lord Jesus, the great shepherd of the sheep, by the blood of the eternal covenant" (Heb. 13:20). The Letter to the Hebrews does not apply the title "priest" to the leaders, or heads, of the community of which it speaks (Heb. 13:7, 17, 24), yet they are associated with the task of preaching and with the Eucharistic meal (Heb. 13:10), and are linked especially with the sacrifice of Christ by their martyrdom (cf. Heb. 13:17).

The Letters of Saint Paul

Just as Jesus never called Himself "priest," so Saint Paul does not identify Jesus with the title, though he surely understands Jesus as a priestly figure through His sacrificial death on the Cross. Christ Himself is the Paschal Lamb who has been sacrificed (cf. 1 Cor. 5:7) and who has rescued us from our sins by this sacrifice (cf. Gal. 1:4). As in the Letter to the Hebrews, Saint Paul emphasizes throughout his writings the uniqueness of the priesthood of Christ, from

which Paul's own ministry flows as a steward of the mysteries of
God (1 Cor. 4:1) and as an ambassador of Christ (2 Cor. 5:20) in
"priestly service of the gospel" through his sanctification by the
Holy Spirit (Rom. 15:15–16). Paul wants to be poured out like a
libation on the sacrificial offering of faith (Phil. 2:17), thereby
administering reconciliation (2 Cor. 5:8). He concludes his Letter
to the Romans by saying, "I have written to you very boldly by
way of reminder, because of the grace given me by God to be a
minister of Christ Jesus to the Gentiles in the priestly service of
the gospel of God, so that the offering of the Gentiles may be
acceptable, sanctified by the Holy Spirit" (15:15–16). In his Letter
to the Philippians, Paul identifies the priestly offering of a bloody
sacrifice with the offering of his own self in the self-offering of Jesus
Christ, saying, "Even if I am to be poured as a libation upon the
sacrificial offering of your faith, I am glad and rejoice with you all"
(2:17). Thus, Saint Paul dares to see his own mission as priestly, in
a way that is "co-extensive with the scope and breadth of the new
priesthood instituted by Christ."[14]

Jesus as Priest, Prophet, and King

The three functions of priesthood—priest, prophet, and
king—though distinct in the Old Testament, are joined in the
New Testament in Christ. When Jesus describes His mission at the
beginning of His ministry, He proclaims, "The Spirit of the Lord is
upon me, because he has anointed me to preach good news to the
poor. He has sent me to proclaim release to the captives and recovering of sight to the blind, to set at liberty those who are oppressed,
to proclaim the acceptable year of the Lord" (Lk. 4:18–19). Added
to this prophetic mission is a supreme authority, so that the Son of
man even has the power to forgive sins (cf. Mk. 2:10). These priestly functions take shape in the images of shepherd and sheep.[15]
Jesus is the Lamb without spot or blemish, offered for the sins of
the world (cf. 1 Pet. 1:19). At the same time, He is the Shepherd,
or Pastor, who sacrifices His life for His sheep (cf. Jn. 6:53). The
authority of Jesus means He serves all, and it is in this way that He

shepherds, refusing any royal understanding of priesthood when others apply it to Him (cf. Jn. 18:36). Instead, Jesus insists on a priesthood in which the one who offers the sacrifice is himself the victim. In this, the unique kingship of the Son of man, which is not of this world (Jn. 18:36), embodies an authority that includes cultic sacrifice and prophetic teaching. Now the prophecy of Psalm 110 is realized as the Son of man is seated at the right hand of the Power (Mt. 26:4); now worship "in spirit and truth" is realized in fulfillment of the prophecy of Jesus that His disciples would eat His body and drink His blood (cf. Jn. 4:23–24, 6:53), sealing a new covenant in His blood for the remission of sins.

Thus, while Jesus refrains from using the title "priest" in its Old Testament sense, He embodies its three functions in another priesthood, which is of the order of Melchizedek.[16] Saint Paul dares to appropriate these functions, as is evident in Acts of the Apostles when the presbyter-bishops of Ephesus are commissioned by the Holy Spirit to feed and guard the flock of Christ (20:26). The priestly people of the New Testament are "a holy nation," called to "a royal priesthood" (1 Pet. 2:9–10), a kingdom of priests (cf. Rev. 5:10); yet certain individuals are set apart for particular priestly ministry to all the rest of the baptized. The Twelve were singled out from among all the other disciples by their commission to baptize (Mt. 28:19), to celebrate the Eucharist (1 Cor. 11:24–5), to forgive sins (Lk. 24:47), and to exercise authority over the rest of the community (Mt. 18:17–18).

The Second Vatican Council

In its Dogmatic Constitution on the Church, *Lumen Gentium*, and in its Decree on the Apostolate of the Laity, *Apostolicam Actuositatem*, Vatican II clearly reaffirms this theology of priesthood, delineating *one* priesthood with its prophetic, priestly, and royal functions, grounded in the priesthood of Jesus Christ. This includes both the priesthood of all the faithful, consecrated through Baptism, and the ministerial or hierarchical priesthood of those consecrated through Holy Orders (LG 10). In *Lumen Gentium*, the

Council goes on to make the point that, while those ordained to the hierarchical or ministerial priesthood "are consecrated to preach the gospel, shepherd the faithful, and celebrate divine worship as true priests of the New Testament," the sacred power of the priesthood reaches its apex in the offering of the Eucharistic sacrifice, in the person of Christ and in the name of the people. Moreover, the Council asserts that the two forms of priesthood differ not only in degree but also in essence (LG 10, 28).

In its Decree on the Ministry and Life of Priests, *Presbyterorum Ordinis*, promulgated on December 7, 1965, by Pope Paul VI, the Council reiterated this teaching and went on to describe priests of the New Testament as those who, "by their vocation and ordination, are in a certain sense set apart in the bosom of the people of God . . . to be totally dedicated to the work for which the Lord has chosen them" (PO 1, 3, 18). This "work" is described in many ways, including as the "work of sanctification"; indeed, this work is not only sanctification of themselves but of the whole Christian community (PO 2, 5–12). Priests in communion with their bishops and with each other work together for all the faithful (PO 7–9). The priestly life is one in pursuit of a perfect likeness to Christ—a holiness reached through nourishing themselves and the people of God with Word and Sacrament (PO 3, 12–13). Therefore, priestly life has special spiritual requirements so that pastoral charity can be animated by humble obedience to God's will, enabled by the right relationship to the things of this world through evangelical poverty and celibate continence (PO 15–17). In order to fully embrace holiness in their vocation, priests are encouraged to draw spiritual nourishment at "the double table of the Sacred Scripture and the Eucharist" and to avail themselves of all the means of spiritual growth—sacramental Penance, spiritual direction and reading, daily examination of conscience, mental prayer and retreats, as well as devotion to the Blessed Mother (PO 18). We will reflect further on these means to priestly sanctity, so often repeated in the Church's teaching on priesthood, in the final chapter of this book.

PRIESTHOOD AND THE CHURCH
Priestly Office

As He had given the Twelve the power to cast out devils (Mk. 3:15), so Jesus commissioned them to preach the Gospel (Mt. 28: 18–20; Mk. 16: 16–18) and linked this commission with the mission to baptize. He empowered them to forgive sins (Lk. 24:47) in the same breath in which He imparted the Holy Spirit (cf. Lk. 24:27; Jn. 20:20–22). As Jesuit Father Jean Galot summarizes: "From all these indications in the gospels we conclude that Jesus meant to impart to the Twelve the total extent of his own pastoral power. He gave them the power to rule the Church, the authority to carry out the mission of evangelization, the power to administer baptism, the power to celebrate the Eucharist and forgive sins. In today's language, Jesus transmitted to the Twelve his own priesthood, which includes leadership, the proclamation of the Word, and the performance of liturgical or sacramental actions."[17]

Gradually, roles in the life of the early Church came to be more clearly delineated, particularly as the twelve apostles began to pass on their charism to successors. Summoning the assembly to solve problems that arose, and after fasting and prayer, they imposed hands upon those chosen for ministry (Acts 6:1–6). This is clearly a "setting apart," a consecration of those chosen through the inspiration of the prophets and teachers. The efficacious response of the Holy Spirit to these gestures is surely a prelude and perfect model of ordination—so that, in this sense, "Pentecost should be looked upon as the prototype of all priestly ordinations."[18]

Among the roles taking shape in the Church, the title of apostle broadened in its significance. James came to be called apostle because of his authority in Jerusalem, which also caused him to be named among the "pillars" of the Church (Gal. 2:9). Saint Luke calls Saul and Barnabas "apostles" after telling how they received the imposition of hands at Antioch (Acts 14:4, 14; 13:1–3). In his letters, Saint Paul uses "apostle" particularly in reference to those who had witnessed an appearance of the risen Lord—the Twelve, James, and then all the apostles, among whom he includes himself

(1 Cor. 15:7). Thus the title is claimed as well by the elder brothers (or presbyters) of the Jerusalem community, since they too had witnessed Jesus' Resurrection.

Saint Paul also names other individuals who held special roles within the Christian community (see 2 Cor. 8:23; Rom. 16:7). The apostles clearly had assistants in the Jerusalem ministry who presided over the Eucharistic "service at tables"—perhaps these were called presbyters (*presbyteroi*), the elders, brothers, or coworkers of the apostles, named at the Council of Jerusalem. Father Galot also suggests that these presbyters may correspond to the seventy-two sent out by Jesus, just as the bishops (*episcopoi*), overseers appointed by the Holy Spirit (Acts 20:28; 1 Pet. 5:1–4), may correspond more to the Twelve and to the other apostles, who would have been the ones to choose the men upon whom they laid hands, as Saint Paul mentions (2 Tim. 1:6; Tit 1:5; Acts 14:23).[19] If such a distinction was not drawn this clearly initially, the eventual differentiation of ministries surely followed this course. The seven chosen to serve at table for the daily service (Acts 6:1–2), usually presumed to be deacons, may actually refer to those ordained to preside over "breaking bread in their homes," which they shared "with glad and generous hearts" (Acts 2:46). The particular needs of the "widows" (Acts 6:1) may accordingly refer to the extension of this daily service to women who lived a consecrated life, set apart for prayer.[20]

In any event, the apostles knew that they had been empowered to impart to others an office they had received from Christ, including the Eucharistic service at tables, requiring prayer and the imposition of hands to "ordain" men for this task. The need for persons to shepherd the flock of Christ in an ongoing way follows the intention of Jesus, for no one knows the time of the end but the Father (Mk. 13:32), and the end of the world will only come after the Gospel has been proclaimed, through trials and persecutions, to all the nations of the earth over a historical extent of time. The necessary gradation of "sacred powers" is rightly called hierarchical, for as Saint Clement, Bishop of Rome, wrote before the end of the first century, the shepherd must watch over the sheep.[21] His predecessor, Saint Peter, describes this shepherd's role, applying it not only to apostles and bishops but to the presbyters as well: "So I exhort the elders among you, as a fellow elder and a witness of the sufferings of Christ. . . . Tend the flock of God that is your charge, not by constraint but willingly, not for shameful gain but eagerly, not as domineering over those in your charge but being examples to the flock" (1 Pet. 5:1–3). Their mission is that of the "chief Shepherd" (1 Pet. 5:4), Christ, who is "the shepherd and guardian [lit. 'bishop'] of your souls."[22]

In this sense, there is always a fundamental distinction between the dignity of the priestly office and the person who carries out its official duties. I can recall the amazement of a young priest who, passing through the church on his way to the sacristy before celebrating Mass, discovered that this congregation followed the practice of rising until the priest had passed by. He expressed his amazement at their respect to the well-seasoned pastor of the church, who simply replied, "Remember son, they didn't rise for you. They rose for the priesthood." The reason for the dignity of the priestly office is the person of Christ, in whom the whole person of the priest is to be consumed—used up in service, in self-renunciation, and even in humiliation. This "depersonalizing" of the priestly office heightens its intimacy:

> The [priestly] office itself is an ecclesiastical-societal form of the presence of Christ, and precisely (as ministry) of the humiliated Christ among those who are his, *a memoria passionis Domini*, "memorial of the Passion of the Lord." . . . The dignity lies in the fact that Christ creates such a transparency in the priest that he, as the one who is totally servant, can let the Lord, who stands above him, become transparent. The more he serves, accordingly, the better does the transparency succeed. . . . In practice, of course, the grace of office has an astonishingly reconciliatory effect in the priest who is humble: that which appears impossible from a human perspective comes as it were automatically, and the power of the promises of Christ shows itself directly to be effective.[23]

Presiding at the Eucharist

Regarding the role of presiding at the Eucharist, Cardinal Avery Dulles observes that while the New Testament does not supply all the details about exactly who in the early Christian community presided at the liturgy, the most priestly activity in the Church, Catholic Tradition has held that the apostles designated bishops, presbyters, or priests to perform this function: "Perhaps in the very early stages, when the permanent structures of the church were still in the process of formation, persons without priestly ordination may have had the capacity to preside at the Eucharist, but if so these practices are not normative for the church of later ages."[24] Cardinal Hans Urs Von Balthasar also describes the clear and irrevocable "boundary line that is drawn in the postapostolic Church between the hierarchical office and the realm of the charisms," which "lies at the point where that which has the force of positive law in the natural society is drawn by her Founder into the supernatural society of the Church in order to be the vessel for his supernatural intentions."[25] Clearly, this development took place rapidly in the early Church as the apostles passed on the apostolic commission and ministry to their successors. Saint Paul does not explicitly mention himself as presiding at the Eucharist, but his ministry of the mysteries of the covenant surely must have included celebration of the Eucharist. Paul solemnly recalls the words of Christ at the Last Supper, and it is his version of these words that more than any other account emphasizes Christ's command: "Do this in remembrance of me" (1 Cor. 11:24–25).[26]

By the end of the first century, the first letter of Saint Clement, Bishop of Rome (a writing contemporary with the last written tradition of the New Testament) already speaks of how the bishops minister to the flock of Christ and piously offer the sacrifices proper to the episcopate.[27] The letter also relates how God "commanded that sacrifices and liturgies be offered, not in a random and irregular fashion, but at fixed times and hours. He has determined, moreover, by His supreme will the places and persons whom He desires for these celebrations. . . . Special ministrations are allotted to the high priest; and for the priests a special role has been assigned; and upon the Levites their proper services have been imposed. The lay person is bound by the rules laid down for the laity."[28] Sulpician Father Raymond Brown sees the threefold symbolism of the Levitical priesthood as being assimilated into the notion of priest in the New Testament, though he recognizes that the Christian pattern of bishop, presbyter, and deacon developed more slowly than Father Galot has suggested, noting that only a century after Saint Clement do we find the term "priest" being applied in a special way to the minister of the Eucharist.[29] In the second century, Saint Ignatius of Antioch insists in his letter to the people of Philadelphia that a Eucharist is not valid unless celebrated by a bishop or someone he appoints: "One is the Flesh of Our Lord Jesus Christ, and one the cup to unite us with his Blood, and one altar, just as there is one bishop assisted by the presbytery and deacons, my fellow servants."[30] By the third century, in his treatise "The Apostolic Tradition," Hippolytus of Rome sees bishops as high priests of worship with a clear primacy over other ministers, such as the presbyters who advise him.[31]

Jesuit Father Christian Cochini asserts that, with respect to "the specific problem of the priestly functions, study of the vocabulary used by the writings of the New Testament shows how the terminology used for the main ranks in the Christian hierarchy is directly borrowed from the Jewish tradition"; thus the words *apostle, bishop, priest,* and *deacon* "have exact equivalents in Hebrew," referring "to Jewish institutions well known by the first Christians."[32] By the third and fourth centuries, presbyters had taken on a greater leadership role in preaching and celebrating the liturgy; it can be taken for granted that by this time the name "priest" designated ordained ministers of the Eucharist, which is the dominant meaning of priesthood in the Church today. As Father Raymond Brown asserts:

Personally, I . . . challenge the notion that a post-NT development [of a cultic priesthood] is a distortion. We Catholics should think of the ordained priesthood as part of our God-given heritage from

Israel, which brought into Christian life the wealth and mystery of the whole area of OT cult. We have managed to preserve, alongside the uniqueness of the sacrifice and priesthood of Christ, the Levitical consciousness of the sacred character of a special priestly service that brings contact with the cultic symbols of God's presence. From this development has come the expectation that a priest be a person of signal holiness and even be expected to live a different style of life.[33]

Thus, Father Raymond Brown also defends the integral connection of the mediating function of the priesthood of the Old Covenant with the priesthood of Jesus Christ. This connection shows that there is *not* a gap between the third-century patristic image of priesthood and that of the apostolic age, but rather a homogeneous development influenced by the Levitical hierarchical pattern.[34] This point is taken up by Vatican Council II in its insistence that, "for the nurturing and constant growth of the People of God, Christ the Lord instituted in his Church a variety of ministries, which work for the good of the whole body" (LG 18). These ministers and their successors, "endowed with sacred power," would serve as "shepherds of His Church even to the consummation of the world" (LG 18, 19). *Lumen Gentium* continues, "In order that the episcopate itself might be one and undivided, He [Jesus] placed Blessed Peter over the other apostles and instituted in him a permanent and visible source and foundation of unity of faith and communion. . . . And for this reason the apostles, appointed as rulers in this society, took care to appoint successors" (LG 18, 20). The Council goes on to point out that priests are coworkers with the bishops, sharing in their own measure in the office of the apostles (PO 2).

Ontological Transformation, Configuration, and Communion

The Second Vatican Council goes on to insist that priests are conformed to Christ the Priest in such a way that they can act in the person of Christ the Head (PO 2). How is this conformation to be understood? Jesus in no way associates Himself with the inherited Jewish priesthood; rather, He is called holy because the Holy Spirit comes upon Mary at His conception (Lk. 1:35). His "holiness is ontological in nature: it is connected with the formation of his human nature, and even more so with the mystery of the Incarnation. Jesus alludes to his holiness when he describes himself as someone 'the Father [has] consecrated and sent into the world' (Jn. 10:36). His consecration coincides with his being sent into the world. This does not mean that it is merely functional: it is a state that exists prior to the activity in which Jesus engages for the sake of salvation. . . . This consecration transcends ritual formalism; it bespeaks a personal commitment."[35]

Like Christ the Priest, the consecration of those who are consecrated in Him is more than functional. Developing through the teaching of Pope Innocent III and the Council of Florence and culminating in the seventeenth-century teaching of the Council of Trent,[36] three sacraments, including the sacraments of Initiation and Holy Orders, were singled out as imprinting an indelible character on their recipient. This means that these sacraments can only be received once, for they involve an "ontological" change of the person in his very being in relationship to Christ and all the members of His Body. Just as one who has been baptized has died with Christ forever, the one who is ordained priest is forever changed in his very being. Beyond any mere functional delegation for service to the Church, he is configured to Christ in a way calling for a permanent and lasting commitment, through a share in Christ's own eternal priesthood.[37] The Council of Trent did not actually determine the precise nature of this sacramental character, but instead restricted itself to affirming it as a spiritual and indelible mark, real and thus ontological. Accordingly, it goes beyond what is merely extrinsic and, surely, beyond a merely juridical empowerment to perform a function.[38]

In his post-synodal apostolic exhortation *Pastores Dabo Vobis*, Pope John Paul II insists upon this "special ontological bond which unites the priest to Christ, High Priest and Good

Shepherd." He points out that this claim was reasserted in the theology of the priesthood found in the teaching of the Second Vatican Council.[39] In his book *Gift and Mystery,* Pope John Paul further observes: "Just as in the Mass the Holy Spirit brings about the transubstantiation of the bread and wine into the Body and Blood of Christ, so also in the sacrament of holy orders he effects the priestly episcopal consecration."[40] The Eucharist is the "food which endures to eternal life, which the Son of man will give to you; for on him has God the Father set his seal" (Jn. 6:27). This perhaps refers to the seal of the Holy Spirit received at Christ's baptism, when the Father certified His beloved Son to do the His work (cf. Jn. 10:33–38), as a consecration for Christ's ministry in the world. This seal, imprinted on the Son by the Father, is in turn imprinted upon those who share His ministry as shepherd.[41] Father Jean Galot explains: "It is well to note that conformity lends to consecration all its reality. Should consecration merely entail surrender to God, without effecting any transformation in the man so surrendered, it would remain extrinsic to the man himself. On the contrary, consecration attains to its full value by effecting the ontological transformation that fashions the person after the divine model."[42]

Benedictine Father Mark O'Keefe aptly describes the force of this understanding of the ontological transformation of the ordained priest: "The priest then is not a 'substitute' or a stand-in for Christ like a proxy at a meeting. Or a substitute teacher in a grade school. The priest makes Christ the Shepherd present in a way similar to the way that the Eucharistic Bread is not just a 'sign' that Christ is present but rather the sacrament of the Eucharist makes Him present in a special way."[43] As Benedictine Archbishop Daniel Buechlein concludes, "The ordinand *is* priest in the person of Christ the High Priest. We are not substitutes. The ministerial priest *does not merely do* priestly things. We are ontologically 'men of the sacred,' as our Holy Father [John Paul II] says."[44]

This "configuration" of the ordained priest to Christ was summed up by Archbishop Daniel Pilarczyk in his own contribution to the 1990 synod on priesthood, as follows: "The priest is a member of the Christian faithful who has been permanently configured by Christ through holy orders to serve the Church, in collaboration with the local bishop, as representative and agent of Christ, the head of the Church, and therefore as representative and agent of the Church community before God and the world."[45] This priestly configuration with Christ lasts throughout the earthly life of the priest, and there is every reason to conclude that, as with Baptism and Confirmation, the permanence of this consecration continues into eternal life.[46]

The introductory chapter of *Lumen Gentium* points out that the mission of the Church involves communion with Christ, the Head of the Body, the Church, and sees the ministerial priesthood as the connection of the whole Church with the headship of Christ. *Lumen Gentium* 28 states that priests exercise "the office of Christ, the Shepherd and Head," and thereby make the actual work of Christ the Head tangible by sharing in His everlasting priesthood. *Presbyterorum Ordinis* elaborates on this notion of the headship of Christ and shows how priests are thus "configured to Christ the priest in such a way that they are able to act in the person of Christ the head" (PO 12). Therefore, priests are called to be "men of communion" through sacramental identification with the eternal High Priest, which inserts the priest, and through him the whole communion of the Church, into the communion of love and life that is the Trinity:

> The priest, "as a visible continuation and sacramental sign of Christ in his own position before the Church and the world, as the enduring and ever-new source of salvation," finds himself inserted into the trinitarian dynamics with a particular responsibility. His identity springs from the *Ministerium Verbi et Sacramentorum,* which is in essential relation to the mystery of the salvific love of the Father [cf. Jn. 17:6–9, 24; 1 Cor. 1:1; 2 Cor. 1:1], to the priestly being of Christ, who personally chooses and calls his ministers to be with him [cf. Mk. 3:15], and to the gift of the Spirit [Jn. 20:21], who communicates to the priest the

necessary power for giving life to a multitude of sons of God, united in the one ecclesial body and orientated towards the Kingdom of the Father. (PDV 12, 16)

Chosen from among Men

The mission given to Christ by His Father requires in turn a multitude of shepherds—shepherds on a pastoral mission bearing the mark of the mission of Jesus. We must conclude that Jesus, while still on earth, shared His mission with His apostles and envisioned even greater numbers of shepherds who would share that mission in the future.[47] Yet there seems to be a "scandal of particularity" in the divine election of these shepherds—in choosing some, God appears to be excluding others. In our own time, this scandal of particularity has arisen over the question of why only men can be ordained.[48] Let us look at the way in which election takes place.

The selection of the Twelve is handed down in such a way as to emphasize how it was the fruit of prayer (Mk. 3:13; Lk. 6:12). Jesus highlights His own role in this choice from among others for this special call to discipleship: "You did not choose me, but I chose you" (Jn. 15:16). The solidarity of Jesus with His chosen ones is identified as their standing by Him faithfully in His trials, and He disposes of the kingdom in their favor, as the Father has disposed of it in favor of the Son (Lk. 22:28–30). While this election to sit on thrones with the power to judge the twelve tribes of Israel (Lk. 6:13, 22:28–30) is from among a large number of disciples, seventy-two others are appointed and sent "ahead of him, two by two, into every town and place where he himself was about to come" (Lk. 10:1). Jesus clearly wills to share His mission to proclaim the Gospel and even to give authority over the powers of evil to the seventy-two disciples as well as to the Twelve.[49]

Despite redefinitions of some priestly functions that may have indeed taken priests off their pedestal and moved them into more collaborative roles,[50] the communion of the priest with the whole Church has an undeniably hierarchical dimension. However much he is a man like everyone else,[51] there is an inescapable aloneness of the priest,[52] which endures even through whatever secularization of the priesthood and which would remain even if celibacy were not a mandatory discipline in the Western Church. The danger of secularized understandings of priesthood lies in suspicion of what is spiritual. Cries that priestly formation has been too "monastic" and now must be secularized often relegate intense prayer and conversion to merely subsidiary roles, disregarding the supernatural power that is essential to any vocation, and surely to priestly vocation. This leads to a tendency to diminish certain essential elements of priestly life, such as the sacramental, ascetic, and contemplative, in favor of a more pastoral ministry that emphasizes preaching.[53] Indeed, the communion given to the Body of Christ is at once a supernatural gift and a continuing task over which the priest has a shepherding role. In order to fulfill this role, the priest is set apart for particular grace—which does not mean that he is better than anyone else but that, having been ordained, he is different. Just as it is impossible to ever fully understand why those three apostles were selected from the Twelve to witness their Lord transfigured, and later were again mysteriously selected to pray nearer to their agonizing Lord in the garden, so is the vocation to the priesthood mysterious. In the face of issues regarding priestly life—which may need to be considered more candidly and honestly—to look at priesthood in a purely naturalistic way is to fail to penetrate to its unchanging heart and to lose sight of its unchanging face, which is the very face of Christ.

The one baptized sacramentally is baptized into the death of Christ, so as to share in His Resurrection. Thus, that one becomes irreversibly a sharer in the common priesthood of the faithful. The indelible mark upon the one baptized and confirmed is eternally the sign of how that one is sealed for Christ. The one ordained sacramentally shares in the eternal priesthood of Jesus Christ in a way that is essentially different from the common priesthood of the faithful; the one ordained priest now acts *in persona Christi capitis,* acts in the very person of Christ, who is the Head of the

Body of which all the faithful are members.[54] Even in this age of
egalitarianism, it is important to recognize this headship of Christ,
lived out by the priest as shepherd, by which the priest truly is
leader of the community.[55] In his encyclical on liturgy, *Mediator
Dei,* Pope Pius XII quotes Saint John Chrysostom, saying that the
priest gives his hand and lends his tongue to Christ.[56] Nowhere is
this seen more effectively than when the priest speaks, in the
person of Christ, the words of Christ at the Last Supper in the
celebration of the Eucharist: "This is my body which is given for
you. Do this in remembrance of me" (Lk. 22:19).

Communion and Trinity

Changed in the depths of his being so that he acts and speaks
in the person of Christ, the priest shares in a particularly intimate
relationship with Christ and through Christ with the beloved
Father, in the power of the Holy Spirit, who is the gift of divine
love in person. These are personal relationships that, far from
being abstract, are *more* real than any relationship with another
human person. Yet, like all relationships, the relationship
between Christ and the priest must be developed and nourished
through priestly ministry and life—a life lived in total self-giving,
together with the self-gift of Christ, renewed constantly through
the Eucharist and deepened in a loving communion of prayer. As
the priest is a man of communion, that communion must first
and foremost be grounded in the source of all communion, in our
one God, who is a communion of three Persons. It is impossible
to build community in the Church or anywhere else if one does
not partake of the profound reality of that communion in God.
The priest must be a man of prayer; only in prayerful communion with the Trinity will anything else about his priesthood
make sense, either on a supernatural or natural level. Only then
can we rightly understand what is changing in the priesthood by
gazing into its unchanging heart—the unchanging heart of the
person of Christ, in whom the priest now lives and acts from the
depth of his being.

It is so much easier to study priesthood, to think about it, rather than to live it; likewise, one can study or think about God without ever beginning to pray to Him. The type of man called to the priesthood is often the intellectually gifted, who uses those gifts well (perhaps too well). I propose this at the outset: *whatever crisis of soul can be diagnosed in priests and in the priesthood is usually a symptom of the failure to enter into the unchanging heart of Christ.* Acknowledging that the priest undergoes a transformation by his ordination, that in the depth of his being he is now in the person of Christ, acting and speaking through an ontologically changed relationship with Christ in his priesthood, takes nothing away from the common priesthood of all the faithful, who are also called by Baptism into communion with Christ as members of His Body.

There is no room for vainglory in priestly consecration. To be set apart in this way is to serve all the rest rather than to be served by them. The mystery of this vocation lays a tremendous responsibility upon the priest. Set apart as he is, his life will never again be his own as it had seemed to be before.

CHAPTER TWO

The
SERVANT
HEART
of the
PRIEST

SERVANT AND CULT

Since he shepherds in the person of Jesus, the Good Shepherd, the priest must be solicitous for the lost sheep, ready even to lay down his life for them if necessary. Jesus drew upon the "suffering servant" songs in the Book of Isaiah to describe the sacrifice required by the servant who gives up his life in atonement (Is. 53:10). Yet in Christ, the "sacrifice of expiation has been transferred from the ritual to the personal sphere."[1] Jesus even shows how this sacrifice is inherent in His very being: "No one takes [my life] from me, but I lay it down of my own accord. I have power to lay it down, and I have power to take it up again; this charge I have received from my Father" (Jn. 10:18).

In his book *The Changing Face of the Priesthood: A Reflection on the Priest's Crisis of Soul,* Father Donald Cozzens, former rector of Saint Mary's Seminary in Cleveland, wonders if a cultic notion of priest diminishes the servant dimension. He feels that "a growing number of priests" have been inspired by the "spirit and vision" of Pope John XXIII and the conciliar documents to come to a "different vision" of ministry and priestly identity than they had found in the cultic mode of priesthood—a mode that once captured the hearts of many aspirants to the priesthood with images of "the priest as mediator between God and human beings; the provider of the sacraments; the guardian of sacred space and sacred truth."[2] Father Cozzens agrees with Jesuit Father Thomas Rausch that priestly identity should evolve toward a model of priest as "servant-leader," calling for the rejection of the title "priest" or any other name that would suggest that "the priest is over the Church or prior to the Church rather than a part of it."[3] This "more holistic" and "authentic" priestly identity involves a shift in emphasis: instead of focusing upon "saving souls through pastoral care and the celebration of the sacraments," which is the "primary function of the priest from the perspective of the cultic model," attention is now to be placed upon "the communal dimension of salvation," in which the "people of God are redeemed and saved as a *people*."[4] For Father Cozzens, the solution is to place an even greater emphasis on the social aspects of the Gospel, such as liturgy: "For so many priests, the identity issue dissolves when they enter into the assembly for worship and prayer. For only in the assembly of the faithful, in the midst of their sisters and brothers in Christ and the Spirit, do they fully experience their role as servant-leader and glimpse, with the rest of the faithful, the grace of their identity in the unfailing mercy and love of God."[5]

It seems to me problematic to suggest that a priest is deprived of seeing himself as "servant" if he "cultically" provides the sacraments and celebrates the liturgy in the role of mediator between God and that assembly of the faithful. The Lord Jesus Himself washed the feet of His disciples on the same occasion when He performed the sacred act of giving His Body and Blood, and both together are to be repeated, following Christ's example in memory of Him. It seems that "scholarly attention" to the present state of priestly identity (which Father Cozzens cites as having achieved what scholarly attention so often does) has given us a bifurcation that splits priestly identity into "cult" and "servant," which the Church's traditional understanding of priesthood has always refused to do. Father Cozzens' love for the dyads of archetypal psychology do not serve him well, seeming to leave him everywhere with bifurcations of the Church's understanding of priestly identity. Thus he is convinced that "ego-inflation and hubris" often cause priests to emphasize the "superior pole of the archetype" in a way that breaks apart the dialectic of such archetypal dyads as "doctor/patient; teacher/student; king/subject; priest/parishioner."[6] According to Father Cozzens, this means that "arrogance and elitism" replace true healing; that "the transforming ecstasy of learning," which protects what is "holy and sacred in the educational process," turns into a "contest of wills"; and that "the inherent mutuality of the members of a local church" fails to flourish because the ordained priest forgets that, though "addressed as 'Father,' he is nonetheless son and brother,"[7] a member of the assembly of the faithful. Though Father Cozzens recognizes that it is increasingly rare for priests to be over-idealized by their parishioners, he urges priests to "come to treat both praise and criticism with a certain indifference," to be "at home with themselves," to "come to terms with their own demons," and not to lose their "heart or their nerve" so that they will discover "their *truth*," that "core of being where the mystery of grace in the midst of the faithful, confirms in wordless and image-less silence their call to priestly service."[8]

Cardinal Hans Urs von Balthasar, following the inspiration of the mystic Adrienne von Speyer, transcends bifurcation and sees the complementarity of mission in the life of the Church. Starting from her earliest days, Mary's interiority, comprehensible only in light of the Cross as being love, reveals the hidden, nuptial consciousness of the Church—the complementarity of the Church of Office, represented by Saint Peter, and the Church of Love, represented by Saint John, who stands at the foot of the Cross in the place of Peter and receives the Marian, faithful Church on his behalf.[9] Though the cultic dimensions of priesthood have surely been overemphasized in the life of the Church at various moments of her history, the solution is not to emphasize social action and liturgy by diminishing the "cultic" aspects of sacrament and sacrifice, as if these interests preclude any real sense of service in priesthood. Rather than a secularized spirituality of the priesthood, it is precisely a *theology* of priesthood that emphasizes the ontological nature of the ordained priest's relationship with Jesus the Priest and is best able to show how the service and sacramental dimensions of priesthood are one. This relationship with Christ is so intimate that the entire being of the priest is given over to living life in a way identical to the way in which Jesus lived it, as a total gift of self-emptying love. Here servant and cult, Word and Sacrament are one. Here communion with the Spirit and with the self-emptying Christ are one. Here the commitment of self, calling for a life-long perseverance in self-gift that is one with the way of total childlike simplicity, blends inseparably in a real relationship, in real communion, with the very person of Christ.

POWER, AUTHORITY, AND INTEGRITY

The proper exercise (rather than the abuse) of power is surely one of the most fundamental and perennial problems that has faced the exercise of authority in the Church. Any exercise of authority in the Church could be seen as objectionable if the Gospel is seen as proposing an ideal of total equality free from any structure, especially hierarchical. Moreover, the need to submit to authority in the Church could be seen as limiting the movement of the Spirit. Yet Jesus Christ exercised power and, tracing His authority to its source, to His heavenly Father, He then authorized His apostles to exercise authority in His name.

Grave problems arise in the life of the Church when worldly power is confused with the power authorized by Jesus Christ, the power of self-giving love. Power is abused unless it is exercised by one who has the authority to do so, or by one who is under authority and exercises it out of the being *(exousia)* of the one who authorizes *(auctoritas,* or author, source). Power in the Church as authorized by Jesus Christ is a totally unique kind of power in that it is a ministry of service and of self-emptying love. So radically is this the case that one could wonder whether authority exercised in the name of Jesus Christ actually consists in being power*ful* or power*less?* In fact, as such great shepherds as Saint Augustine and Saint Gregory the Great realized, alongside the improper exercise of power is a *failure* to exercise power: a failure of the shepherd to truly watch over his flock, a failure to exercise his pastoral ministry, which may jeopardize the very welfare of the flock.

Ultimately, Christ is the Lord and the living Law of His Church. His authority flows from within the self-emptying love among the Persons of the Trinity.[10] The *Directory for the Life and Ministry of Priests* elaborates on both the hierarchical and communal dimensions of priesthood, within the fundamental understanding of the priest as a man of communion. The priest as servant is not contradicted by the royal meaning of priest, especially if the priest keeps a prayerful heart focused on the meaning of the kingship of Jesus Christ. In fact, to set charism in opposition to institution has a *dis*integrating effect on priestly identity. In Church Tradition and in the teaching of Vatican Council II, the priest is a man of communion, in collaboration with the bishop, and "in the individual local communities of the faithful makes the Bishop present, so to speak, to whom they are united with a faithful and great spirit" (LG 28; cf. PO 7; cf. PDV 17).[11] Ideally, the bishop should be *episcopus* in the true sense of looking over (not overlooking) everything. He should be in a position to take in the big picture, and he will need to collaborate in order not to become myopic. He should have in view all of the needs of the Church and ultimately have a missionary heart and mind.[12] As is shown by the Crucifixion of Jesus Christ and by the experiences of those who have been called to a ministry of leadership, exercising authority in the Church is a hazardous enterprise. It involves an empowerment that does not always simply correspond to calculable or identifiable natural gifts or dispositions, or to measurable preparedness. Indeed, the first disciples were not given much of an orientation before the Lord sent them forth, giving them authority over unclean spirits, an authority given out of the very being (*exousia*) of Jesus Himself: "The one who hears you, hears me; the one who despises you, despises me" (Lk. 10:16).[13]

Thus, there is indeed a fundamentally hierarchical structure to priestly ministry in the Church. As Cardinal Hans Urs von Balthasar points out:

The priest should announce that he has genuine authority vis-à-vis the faithful and that he should receive genuine obedience from them, but he should understand and present this genuine authority as the authority of Jesus Christ by behaving only as their "servant." . . . The central difficulty for the priestly man is how he can make his personal love transparent to the obedient love of Christ and make what is an impersonal legal attitude at the same time credible as Christian brotherly love. He must not bind in a personal manner to himself the fellowman whom he loves but must lead him by way of a genuinely human relationship of brotherly love to the love of Christ.[14]

Indeed, the abuse of power comes when it is not grounded in the one who authorizes it but in the one who wields it. The discomfort in our times with any verticality of structure, especially in the life of the Church, can perhaps be partially attributed to abuses of power that have that have taken place within the Church; yet a rejection of authority sometimes conceals a covert fascination with power, subverting hierarchical authority only to establish the power of the one attempting to overthrow it. Passive-aggressive behavior, by being helpless, inert, or simply immovable, can render authority powerless while seeming to respect it. Often, a priest will decry as oppressive any exercise of authority or legislation on the part of his bishop, while jealously guarding his own authority in his "fiefdom." As an antidote to ambition, and to avoid misunderstanding power and authority in the Church, it is well to remember that from the very beginnings of the Church we Christians have had a history of "crucifying" those who try to lead us.

Let us immediately and unequivocally decry all abuse of authority and power, whether inside the Church or outside it, that is arbitrary or self-serving rather than humbly seeking to serve others in a selfless way. Let us at the same time promote a genuine love and respect for those who hold office in the Church, offices provided for by the hierarchical structure of the Church. In order to live a truly collaborative life in the Church, including in her ministry, it is not necessary to overthrow all hierarchy, making everything horizontal. It is not necessary to make every role in the Church the same as every other role, to declericalize the clergy and to clericalize the laity, in some well-intended but misguided effort to pervasively "democratize" the Church.[15]

If we look carefully at priestly identity as Church Tradition has faithfully transmitted it, we find that the exercise of authority is not in competition but rather is intimately integrated with service. It does not contradict but calls for a hierarchical dimension. The priest is called to assume the role of head in the life of the Church, "placing himself *in front of* the Church . . . being a guide who works toward the sanctification of the faithful entrusted to his ministry, which is essentially pastoral. This reality, which has to be lived with humility and coherence, can be subject to two opposite temptations. The first is that of exercising this ministry in an overbearing manner, while the second is that of disclaiming the configuration to Christ Head and Shepherd because of an incorrect view of community."[16] The distinction between the common and ministerial priesthood is best served by realizing how the hierarchical communion of the whole Church, the *ordo presbyterorum* in which the ordained priest is inserted, preserves the communion of the whole Church—a hierarchical subordination for the sake of communion,[17] rather than as its antithesis. The need to achieve identity by the elimination of difference is fundamentally dis-integrating, because, as Balthasar writes:

> No Christian has any privilege vis-à-vis another Christian at this innermost point, since even the vocation of the apostles does not stand "higher" than any one of the baptized; this means also that the original baptismal mission of the layman cannot be derived as a delegation from the clerical authority, since it is subordinate to this authority only at a secondary stage as the body that is competent in all matters of Church order. But this means that the original baptismal mission of the layman is not to be understood as a "right," any more than we were willing . . . to see the commission of the apostles to preach as a "right" vis-à-vis the peoples.[18]

Father Donald Cozzens denounces the "the sexual/celibate/ power systems that presently define the priesthood and episcopacy," which are intolerant of discussions that "may lead to insights into the negative aspects of the clerical system that may be creating an atmosphere or a set of circumstances that in turn foster the kinds of behaviors at the core of the present crisis."[19] Referring to one of the greatest challenges facing the priesthood and the Church, he points out the "need to determine if the systemic structure of the clerical culture and world is unwittingly attracting individuals at risk for misconduct with minors, and we need to determine if the priesthood's systemic structure itself encourages and fosters healthy spiritual and emotional growth in its members." But Father Cozzens also fears that "the kind of study and analysis the present crisis calls for will prove too threatening in the present climate of suspicion and mistrust."[20]

While there are negative aspects to "the clerical system" in much need of reform, I hope to show that the reform needed is much more fundamental than eliminating a Church discipline regarding celibacy or stripping priests of the power to shepherd. Reform, in fact, must go in the other direction—not relaxing or eliminating the discipline, but recovering the evangelical counsel *beneath* the discipline, *renewing* the power of the priesthood and the authority of the Church by reforming the exercise of these functions, so as to allow Christ-like, self-sacrificing love to be lived more authentically. The problem of power and authority will never be resolved by simply demanding to be heard, for often the complaint of not being listened to hides a very different one: the complaint that I was heard but did not get what I wanted. Discipline can change, especially in order to retrieve its deeper meaning, but unwillingness to compromise Church teaching is not an abuse of power. To generalize upon those instances where power truly is being abused by calling them "systemic," and to go on to blame the problem on the fact that the "system" is celibate or clerical, is to miss the point entirely.

Power to Know

Faithfulness to the Church does not call for the suppression of the desire or ability to think or to know, but presumes them. Surely the role in the life of the Church assumed by any baptized member entails an added responsibility for living and handing on the faith to others.[21] The need for priests to remain engaged in ongoing, serious, and prayerful study cannot be overstated: priests who study regularly pray differently. Prayer and study are essential parts of the responsibility of the ordained priest, by virtue of his office or order, to the members of the common priesthood of all the faithful. The only way to hand on the faith in a way that is at once prophetic and faithful is to do so within the communion of the Church, joined to the communion of those ordained in the succession of the apostles. This is the only way in which all the faithful can be empowered with the knowledge of the full truth. There are real complexities in this and in other areas of priestly life where personal faith and identity can clash with the office a priest has in the communion of the Church. If a priest can no longer in good conscience proclaim the Gospel as it is handed on in the Tradition of the Church, he surely needs to struggle for the full truth; if the conflict of conscience persists, he may need to withdraw altogether from the exercise of his priestly ministry. Structural and institutional aspects of the Church can seem obstructive and may lead to disillusionment for a priest or for anyone trying honestly to settle his conscience. In his position as spiritual leader, the priest is in a position where he might begin, too facilely, to see himself as the "persecuted prophet," defending the rights of the marginalized, and perhaps even seeing the attempts of the Magisterium to shepherd the Body of Christ as self-serving. Rather, his ability to think and know should be actively engaged in the service of discovering more and more dimensions of the truth, communicating these in fruitful solidarity with the rest of the Church.

If one's convictions contradict what the Church teaches, one's integrity is at stake. The Church has continued to uphold certain teachings, such as her teaching on sexuality. If "a wide variety of well-informed, religiously concerned, honest, and sincere people do not accept the official Church teaching about sex" and even "reject the basic rationale on which ecclesiastical judgments have been formulated,"[22] is the integrity and credibility of Church teaching preserved by accommodating those who cannot accept her teaching, or does it lie in steadfast adherence to the truth? These are challenges that every priest faces, and that challenge becomes even greater if "many of those who represent or promulgate the Church's official teaching about sex do not themselves abide by it."[23]

To make a norm of the conflicts that may be met in the exercise of priestly office is to start out with a bifurcation that splits priestly identity as it shatters the communion of the Church. To make much of abuses or misuses of power by members of the hierarchical communion of the Church, and to make these abuses appear as the norm, likewise leaves us with shattered communion and makes subjectivism seem the only way to preserve personal integrity. Such an approach actually fosters abuse of power by seeing all authority as the enemy. Those who constantly feel the need to question every authority create at least as much of a problem as those who feel it should never be questioned. Many priests who claim to have been "liberated" from the "enslavement" of unquestioning obedience to their bishops and superiors remain tyrants themselves over those under their authority. Often, despite their claim to have been liberated from a preoccupation with power, and therefore willing to shed all power and to participate in open collaboration with everyone, an honest assessment can show that the terms of disclosure and collaboration can be quite selective; I may be all too happy to collaborate only with those who share my agenda. Often, priests who adamantly maintain their right to follow their own conscience and to pursue their own personal discernment resist any dialogue that could challenge the conclusions they have already reached, especially if that dialogue is with someone in authority. When I hear a priest loudly assert over and over again how little he cares about or is immune to any influence of his bishop or other Church authority, I start to wonder if he "protesteth too much," especially when he seems to remain obsessed with what he sees as the misuse of power on the part of those in authority and needs over and over again to uncover such "abuses."[24]

Power and Compromise

Just as Jesus passed His authority on to the apostles and continues to shape that authority as it is passed on to the Church, so the nature of our relationships to our own parents influences and shapes our relationships later in life. Just as one might see parental dynamics at work in the relationship that a married person has with his or her spouse and children, so too one might detect residual parental issues in the relationship of a priest to the Church. Often, these parental influences upon subsequent relationships are beneficial, but they always bring some limitations. Occasionally, they can even impede mature adult relationships, paralyzing them or dooming them to regression or repetition of earlier impasses in love and trust.

Because they vow obedience, priests are not necessarily any more likely than married people to fall prey to early parental patterns of relating. Married persons also vow a mutual submission. It has been my experience through my clinical work counseling seminarians and priests, and also working with many other married and unmarried persons, that strengths and deficits are bequeathed and distributed rather evenly across the board. At the present time, marriage and family life are widely devastated by instability and self-centeredness. This scars the rest of society in ways similar to how it has scarred many of those coming into seminaries. It can be tempting to compromise on many fronts: while some might be tempted to pursue priesthood as an easy way of gaining identity and security, others are tempted to move in with a lover or find a niche in the corporate world as a way of getting a "quick fix." The "normality" of married life can also be appealing and used as an escape from one's own problems.

I have often found that the conversion and discernment process leading to entering seminary and growing into priestly ministry actually matures men who respond to this vocation at an extraordinarily greater rate than one finds in their peers who pursue other vocations. If being a "son of the Church" could keep a certain priest a child, entrenching him in an infantile posture as if he is a "kept" man, it frees most others for a greater autonomy. A genuine leaving of father, mother, home, and family leads to embracing celibacy not for self-gratification or for "what it can do for me,"[25] but as an honest and responsible posture of self-giving. It is possible in any way of life to become suspended in an adolescent posture, suspicious of any authority, needing to be "me" in an uncompromising way, and never making any lasting commitment except to my own freedom to change my mind.

Compromises of integrity can be manifold. It is possible for a priest to compromise his mind, his heart, or his conscience in ways that destroy his identity as a priest and as a man. While some systems of priestly formation have prevented resolution of underlying conflicts and have perpetrated disintegrating compromise, it is another thing entirely to imply that faithful submission to authority and adherence to commitments made earlier in life incline one toward lasting compromises of personal integrity. As Bishop Earl Boyea, former rector of the Pontifical College Josephinum, asserts:

> To be sure, I have felt at times, a tension between Church teaching and my own pastoral sensibilities when working with the real problems of people. I take that as a signal that I need to understand the teaching more thoroughly. Let me say it quite flatly: my presumption is not that I am right but that the Church is right. Christ made no individual promise to me that the Spirit would lead me into all truth; he did not give me the keys of the kingdom. These are promises made to the Church, the Body of Christ, of which I am a member not as an equal but as a servant.[26]

It is dangerous to serve up a tossed salad of disillusionment and compromise and attribute it to one source. There can be many reasons why a person has shut down or has found that his heart and energy lie elsewhere than his earlier commitment.[27] The source of the priest's energy is the source of the authority of priestly office, Jesus Christ. This energy comes from the mission among the Persons of the Trinity, a mission from the Father and given by the Son, Jesus, to His apostles. Expressed most profoundly in the "Eucharistic surrender," the life-giving power of this mission surges through subsequent generations of believers, through a historical continuity. It is this mission, this permanent feature of the Church and of its priesthood, which grounds her authority:

> The missioning of the apostles by Christ is a special act, clearly set apart from the identities given to all other believers; for Christ extends his mission in a special way to them. . . . The Twelve were specially endowed with the authority to form the foundation of the Church and were for that reason equally expropriated and called to join in Christ's sacrificial existence. And this expropriation means that their identity was emptied for the sake of the Eucharist.[28]

We have already mentioned that while power can be exercised in a way that is abusive, the failure to exercise power can also be an abuse. When the American cardinals gathered in Rome in April 2002 to discuss the scandal of clergy sexual abuse, Pope John Paul II pointed out that child abuse is part of a larger crisis caused by an amoral attitude towards human sexuality, its "prime victims" being "the family and the young."[29] Calling for a complete examination of the causes and for the "conversion" of those living in this sin, the pope went on to say,

> It must be absolutely clear to the Catholic faithful, and to the wider community, that Bishops and superiors are concerned, above all else, with the spiritual good of souls. . . . They must know that Bishops and priests are totally committed to the fullness of Catholic truth on matters of sexual morality, a truth as essential to the renewal of the priesthood and the episcopate as it is to the renewal of marriage and family life. . . . Be confident that this time of trial will bring a purification of the entire Church, a

purification that is urgently needed. . . . So much pain, so much
sorrow, must lead to a holier priesthood, a holier episcopate, and
a holier Church.[30]

This admonition of Pope John Paul was incorporated in the
Charter for the Protection of Children and Young People, formulated and approved in 2002 by the United States Conference of
Catholic Bishops at its meeting in Dallas. The test of this charter's
effectiveness and its subsequent evaluation and revision must recognize that it is an abuse of episcopal power to fail to look over, and
instead to overlook, problems that exist in the Church—to stall in
bringing about their resolution or to become more preoccupied
with political correctness than with the truth. After the bishops'
conference in Dallas, it will become much harder to overlook the
sexual misconduct of priests. But is it not also a failure to exercise
episcopal power and authority to reduce the implementation of *Ex
Corde Ecclesiae*, for example, to a "private matter" between a bishop
and a theologian, leaving the faithful in the dark about whether col-
leges and universities are truly carrying out their Catholic mission?
Pastors of parishes also can look the other way when their schools or
religious education programs are being directed by persons who are
pursuing an agenda other than that of the Church, or are staffed by
teachers who either do not know the faith or who promote their
own opinion. It is as much a failure on the part of a bishop to move
a priest to another parish after he has disrupted a congregation by
dissenting from Church teaching from the pulpit as it is to transfer
to another parish a priest who has engaged in sexual misconduct.

Power and Loss

We have already observed that power has to do not only with
having and taking, but also with giving and surrendering. Its affinity with loss is therefore assured. Priests have to let go of a lot in
order to follow their vocation, and they must be free to grieve their
losses. Perhaps in a more poignant way than before, priests must
give up and grieve the loss of exercising unquestioned authority (if

they even ever felt that they had such a power). Nevertheless, they should not need to give up the confidence people place in them by virtue of their vocation. *There is a significant difference between grieving over what I have lost and grieving over what I will never have.* When priests "have lost confidence in their chanceries and seminaries" because the "best of bishops and chancery staffs can be caught in the grip of institutional paralysis and denial,"[31] perhaps what has to be grieved is the loss of an idealized sense that bishops and chanceries have all the answers. On a personal level, perhaps I have to grieve the fact that not even I will ever know what is best and that I may even lose my faith in prayer by trying to find all the answers analytically.

Father Cozzens has an interesting perspective on what he calls the "presbyteral Oedipal complex,"[32] which defines an Oedipal triangle of the newly ordained priest-son, the idealized bishop-father, and the mother-Church who wants her son totally for herself. Often a priest may need to let go of the expectation that his self-gift to the Church will always be favored with the best assignments within this unique presbyteral brotherhood, if only he waits and obeys. Such a "pre-Oedipal bliss" eventually has to give way so that the priest can let go of and grieve the fact that he might never become a bishop and ascend to full fatherhood in that idealized way. Yet this "complex" delineated by Father Cozzens means that the developmental goal of priesthood is once again bifurcated. As the priest establishes "his own identity as an individual distinct from his family," he suffers "the anxiety and tension of being loyal to the Church and faithful to his own vision." Father Cozzens claims that there are those priests who "cannot bear to stand in the fire leading to true adulthood" and who find that the "tension and accompanying ambivalence found in standing both as a man of the Church and their own man is too much." Such priests "follow one of two false paths: either becoming sycophant ecclesiastics and pious, effete clerics or the less common but equally destructive path of the maverick." According to Father Cozzens, such presbyteral and episcopal

Oedipal complexes intermesh, and the priest hopes that "the approval of his father-bishop and . . . the symbiotic union with his mother-Church . . . can . . . assuage the anxiety and restlessness of his soul," quieting the "unruly urges of his sexuality with the erotic fulfillment of clerical power and status."[33]

Undoubtedly, there are such individuals as Father Cozzens describes; every chancery or diocese has a few. But there are still more widespread and pervasively devastating effects caused by other perduring, unconscious conflicts, such as those manifested in the never-satisfied carping about the directives coming from bishops "downtown," for which priests are notorious. Is this incessant and emotional obsession actually a refusal to truly grieve over that idealized father-figure who will never be? Continuing to complain about everything while denying the real source of disappointment, grounded in ambition or otherwise, may leave a priest mired in negativity, cynicism, and even bitterness. It is such unresolved conflict, pervasive among the rank and file of priests, which has created a climate that causes many priests to avoid clerical gatherings as too "demoralizing" and which has done much more than ambition alone to maintain immature relationships in the priesthood and to destroy communion in the Church.

Bishop Robert Lynch writes openly of the "fragility of the diocesan priesthood" and the difficulties from the side of the bishop in his collaboration with his priests. Bishops, too, have to let go of thinking they must be capable of solving every problem.[34] But do priests ever let go of their ideal expectations of their leaders in a way that allows this? Can the priest enter into the efforts his bishop is making to listen compassionately while he needs at the same time to make decisions and take action? Do priests who lament the inability of their parishioners to understand the quandaries they face in their role as pastor at the same time fail themselves to understand the quandaries their bishop might face when presented with the "whole picture," as he sees it as the *episcopus*?

There is, then, a lot to let go of, and much over which to grieve. Father Cozzens mentions with pathos reading of "a priest once who, sitting alone late one night in the kitchen of his rectory, heard himself utter aloud, 'God takes no pleasure in this loneliness.'" In light of this, Father Cozzens asks, "What crosses have we placed on our priests that are not ordained by God? What structures, customs, and disciplines keep too many of them immature and anxious?"[35] Surely structures, customs, and disciplines do need to be constantly examined—failure to do so has heavy consequences. Yet there is *unchanging truth* at the heart of the Church and at the heart of the priesthood, of which customs and structures are only reflections. If customs and structures are to be reformed, we must look to this deeper heart in order to understand celibacy and celibate aloneness.

Richard Sipe speaks of this celibate aloneness while analyzing "the paradox of love and loneliness." Since loneliness is part of the human condition, Sipe argues, it is naive to reflect upon the loneliness of priesthood without also recognizing that loneliness is also a part of marriage and parenthood.[36] All vocations require a willingness to accept loss, for loneliness is "the price we pay for love, consciousness, and self-consciousness."[37] Whatever benefits accrue to the priest from institutional loyalty, *esprit de corps*, or even from power and ambition do not eliminate the need to face loss and gain, and do not spare the priest "a trace of depression at the time of initial awareness of [his] celibate destiny."[38] In fact, the very "ability to begin the celibate process is dependent on some awareness of loss and gain." Being aware of a separateness from most of the people one ministers to, one may be overwhelmed by a sense of isolation, realizing that, as a priest, "I am not like other men."[39]

This awareness is very different from the process Father Cozzens describes as sustaining an invincible identity as *puer aeternus*,[40] the eternal child. All must fall, sooner or later, from the pedestal of narcissistic self-adulation or elitism. The internalization of celibacy and of priestly identity—which according to Richard Sipe's calculations comes at about thirteen or eighteen years into celibate life—requires a resignation to being different, leading to a consolidation of priestly identity.[41] This is the opposite of the desperateness that can be found among celibates and non-celibates alike, an overeagerness "to connect with anyone willing to show some sign of affection and acceptance."[42] This desperation can come from a pervasive loneliness, a desperate attempt to escape loneliness, and the experiences of absence, loss, and separation. But "loneliness" can be transformed into "aloneness" when I am able to accept the reality of still being in relation with those who are not immediately available to me, those who may be gone but with whom I am still in union. This acceptance allows me to realize who I am, even as I am alone, as well as who others are and who God is. As Sipe concludes: "The realization and acceptance of who we are, and who God is, is felt and savored in aloneness. Think about that word 'aloneness': It can be parsed ALL-ONE-NESS. This is what is on the other side of pain, sacrifice, and self-knowledge of loneliness—the reality that we are all one."[43]

For the celibate as well, loneliness, like fear, becomes more potent when we avoid it. Until we can face the inevitable loneliness that celibate love involves, we have not even begun the process of becoming celibate. Attempts to avoid or escape loneliness perpetuate endless cycles of overwork, distractions, negativity, or just noise—all of which are fatal to priestly identity and growth. Such distractions deprive the priest of the silence and the solitude in which he can meet Christ in a personal relationship, which enables him to meet Christ in every other relationship of his life and ministry. We are all one, but each must realize this truth one person at a time, or as Mother Teresa said, "one Jesus at a time." To do so, I must surrender my desire to find a definitive escape from all loneliness, which I will never achieve this side of death. In being alone but not being afraid of aloneness, I can let go of fear and accept a solitude from which I can truly be in relationship with God and with others. I have to let go of loss and gain in order to receive the gift of the "other," and I must offer the gift of myself, which allows relationship.

Power and Sexuality

Clearly, there are profound connections between sexuality and power. Cardinal Balthasar describes how the "outwardly directed intentionality" of the "inherently instinctual" sexual drive seeks the power of that "moment of 'deceptive infinity,'" which is false; on the other hand, "the more spiritual love becomes between human beings, the more it will focus on the gift that has been offered to it by the beloved other, and the more it will be inclined (and able) to accept this gift, which for the moment is the appropriate and satisfactory one because it comes from love. Love assures that the lover will not be tempted to look around the gift, trying to find something more fulfilling."[44]

Power can certainly make one "drunk" with a deceptive infinity, which becomes less and less satisfactory as its deception is unmasked, leading to a more and more desperate and even addictive urgency to "take it all" or to "have it all." Love, on the other hand, has a fulfillment that has more to do with giving and taking than with demand and response to that demand. The love of which two human beings are capable, especially in marriage, is

> able to unite a certain inner infinity with a certain external finitude . . . the relation of creature and God: that the primarily feminine and receptive creature can be fulfilled by the all-abundant and all-free God in all sorts of ways that will strike the creature as being all the more satisfactory the more it conquers its thirst for a false intimacy. . . . This attitude of receptivity is essential in order for the creature to allow its powers to "stay awhile" in grateful reception of the divine gift and to experience in this restful contentment that the ever-greater God and the fullness of his gifts have been offered to it.[45]

Abuse of power cannot rest in this contentment, nor can it recognize the ever-greater God, who is the authority behind sexual power. One does not have to adopt all the ramifications of Freud's theory of the life and death instincts to agree with him in recognizing a natural interplay of sexual drives and power.[46] But the fulfillment of human sexuality in intimacy ultimately involves a power that does not need to overpower but is willing to surrender. The urge to overpower can seek to overflow any natural boundaries, pursuing pathways of sexual deviance. In discussing the widespread incidence of the sexual abuse of children, Father Stephen Rossetti points to the fundamental distortion in our society's perceptions of sexuality and aggression.[47] Aggression and hatred can lie deep; the attempt to cope with these and many other deep-seated emotions can become an issue of control, for power over oneself and one's own emotions seems to be assured when power over others is maintained. Sexuality inherently transmits a sense of power and overpowering, which may bring an addictive high and the promise of assured power. The base of this power is in reality so fragile, however, that a cycle of powerlessness alternating with power develops and continues to be played out, over and over again.[48]

Being largely in denial, society enables and even cultivates these distortions, becoming collectively caught up in cycles of addiction. As is usually the case with denial, despite pervasive evidence of the confusion of sexuality and violence in the media and popular culture (a reality also seen in the high incidence of violent sexual crimes), the attitude prevails that this is only normal, recreational, or even healthy. Such denial is sadly enhanced even among the social sciences by the tendency to relativize away any notion of behavioral or sexual deviance. The normalization of the abnormal is perhaps reflected in the preference for substituting the more neutral word "paraphilia" for the term "perversion." If sexuality is our fundamental human capacity to be self-gift, then when power induces or forces another into something sexual we have a fundamental distortion of sexuality that is abusive of the other person. If our sexual capacity to make a gift of ourselves to another is turned into some activity, whether solitary or interpersonal, that perverts or destroys that possibility, it merits the name perversion.

These issues of power, and the possibility of denying the presence and force of power and its misuse, can easily be found within priestly life, rationalizations notwithstanding. We make our own the principle articulated by Richard Sipe that "any and all sexual exchanges between a priest or a dedicated celibate and another violate professional ethics and are therefore not responsible. Sexual contact in any pastoral ministry, teaching, spiritual direction, confession, counseling, supervision, or any church-related activity is inappropriate, irresponsible, and can be reprehensible and criminal—a violation of power and trust."[49] There are many reasons for this: even aside from the morality of such action and the inconsistency between what is being professed and what is being done, the priest is in a position of power, making it easier for him to victimize another. We will discuss momentarily the problems of sexual addictions and dependencies, and the problems of freedom experienced by the sex addict; yet we must insist here that, in any relationship someone has with a priest, the betrayal of trust is most severe in its effects and consequences.

All use of power involves boundaries, and the temptation to abuse power by crossing these boundaries can be even greater when the boundaries are sexual, since the appeal of sexuality lies in its illusive promise of the power to obliterate and transcend all boundaries (the deceptive infinity we discussed earlier). The confusion of power and sexuality in the priesthood constitutes a failure of what is expected preeminently from a celibate priest: "Celibacy in priesthood is a special way of coming to terms with one's own sexuality, of establishing one's own boundaries in service of the community, as a way of loving and living out one's spiritual life."[50] The failure of a priest to live out what is expected of him can simply be the consequence of his personal immaturity, but his victims are more vulnerable because their expectations are higher, due to the higher degree of trust placed in a priest. Thus, Father Rossetti identifies in the sexual abuse of children by an adult a need to feel strong or powerful, and notes how research shows that the most traumatizing element of the sexual abuse of children is not being used as a sexual object, but rather the abuse of trust and power.[51] It would certainly seem that these insights could be extended to any abuse of power, at any age, which violates trust—certainly when someone is victimized by the abuse of priestly power.

Sadly, some may be drawn to priesthood who want to accede to the power built into ordination because they are depleted in their inner sense of their own personal worth, value, and lovableness and have gone on to idealize sexual strength as ways to achieve these. Using sexuality to overpower the powerless is obviously in diametrical opposition to the stance of a follower of Christ, who leads others in following Christ. Yet the powerful position of a priest often makes him unassailable and invulnerable to the conversion that can bring healing and renewal to his priestly life, especially in that typically unmentioned area of his sexuality. While there have been dramatic changes in the way in which priests exercise power, and while collaboration and dialogue certainly leave priests more vulnerable to challenge and criticism in many areas of their ministry, celibacy can still seem to give a priest a special power that is intimately involved with his sexuality.

Ultimately, whether I am celibate, single, or married, no one person can be everything for me. Sexuality inherently promises that someone, that *this* one can, and this promise lies at the heart of the complicated relationship of sexuality and power. The Christian approach to relationships, sexuality, and intimacy does not give up on love because no one person can be everything for another. Neither does Christian love of others give in to the temptation to substitute power for intimacy, or possession and control for relationship. Celibates can truly aspire to give up having any particular "one" for the sake of serving and loving all, yet may still experience strong desires to have "someone." Indeed, they may be even more vulnerable to succumbing to the illusion that *this* particular person can fill me after all. Because of his strong relationship with what is transcendent and otherworldly, a priest may feel entitled to cross all boundaries for the sake of the absolute power with which he has endowed this idealized other person.

We just described some of the loneliness involved in the celibate life of a priest; but there is loneliness in every life, as each one of us has to let go of and grieve over the realization that I will never find a particular "someone" out there who will be everything for me. Authentic priestly celibacy is a gift that aspires to have no one in particular for the sake of being more available to love and to minister to many others. The particular vulnerability in which a priest finds himself, without any particular "other" of his own, is greatly exacerbated by the fact that by his priesthood he is in a position in which people can expect *him* to be everything for them. The aura of transcendent omnipotence that can surround a priest may complicate even more the entanglement of power with sexual feeling. A "spiritual intimacy" can soon appear to take on a privileged quality beyond space and time, making this spiritual relationship seem uniquely special and singular, an exception to every rule and every limit. On whichever side these feelings of omnipotence arise, it can be very tempting for a priest to try to exercise that power with which someone has endowed him or with which he would like to be endowed.

Ultimately, as a celibate, the priest is in a privileged position to love many, to love selflessly, and to witness to the totally, infinitely self-giving love of God, who alone can be everything for us. The *kenosis* of Christ must predominate how a priest loves and ministers, especially in any exercise of power in his priestly office. Ultimately, the priest must cultivate this disposition in all honesty, so as to be open to receive the grace of his vocation and office.

Power and Addiction

Much of what we have already said prepares us to understand how power can propel cycles of addiction. Salesian Father John Harvey defines addiction as patterns of thought and feeling causing behavior in relationships that shows an individual is out of control, meaning that he has had little or no success in his conscious attempts to rid himself of this behavior.[52] The object to which I am addicted promises to fill me up, and thereby takes me away from the only possible human happiness, which comes from *emptying* oneself.

Addictions can be physiological and psychological, and it is probably better to assume the involvement of both these dimensions of the human person in every addiction. The more obvious addictions are substance addictions, such as to drugs or alcohol. More recently, it has been recognized that people can become addicted to other persons, and this too has both physiological and psychological causes and consequences.[53] Genetic research and mapping have attempted to identify the genetic foundations of various addictions; yet whatever genetic predisposition may eventually be demonstrated as a basis for addiction, it must be remembered that it is just that—a pre*disposition* and not a pre*determination.*

Priests have demonstrated their vulnerability to addiction—most notably, to alcohol—and more recently have been recognized as vulnerable to sexual addiction. Sexual addiction can involve actual heterosexual or homosexual sexual contact with someone else, or it may be a compulsive attachment to a person that does not include sexual activity. Moreover, sexual addiction may be autoerotic or may employ pornography or fetishes. (We will deal with the issue of sexual abuse of minors in chapter four.) Sometimes other adults of either sex can also become the focus of obsessive preoccupation and compulsive attachment. Often, a long series of such attachments becomes evident to all while the addict still considers them to be concealed. The anatomy of this "mirror of obsession" becomes evident in patterns of out-of-control behavior, which usually becomes more and more high-risk and self-destructive as the level of activity increases, since the current level becomes insufficient.[54] Alcoholism has been found to have a significant hereditary component, that is, it runs in the family. This probably means that not only are genetic predispositions handed on, but also that these are involved with familial patterns of using and abusing alcohol. What is going on in all addiction is revealed in a more explicit way when substances such as alcohol are abused: there is a desire for the "high," for the sense of well-being and completion.[55] Judgment is impaired, and soon even personality can begin to change or deteriorate as the addiction worsens.

Priests too can demonstrate addictive patterns with respect to substances such as medications or even food and to habits such as work. Addictions can become driven by thirst for power, with its concomitant sense of being in control, even including the search for the "high" brought about by the substance or induced by the experience. For a priest, the quest for the fulfillment of spiritual ideals can have such a lack of tangible results as to create an emptiness, which the addiction then seeks to fulfill.

Formerly, addictions were treated as moral lapses that could be corrected by a transfer, or by a retreat or rest. More recently, under the inspiration of Alcoholics Anonymous, twelve-step programs have sprung up for every conceivable type of addiction: alcohol, narcotics, gambling, overeating, sex, and love.[56] These twelve-step programs enjoy a great deal of popularity and success, and spiritual programs have ensued which build upon the twelve steps.

Dr. Patrick Carnes delineates three behavioral types of addiction: the *arousal* addictions, triggered mainly by the desire for the pleasure of arousal; the *satiation* addictions, which seek the sense of completeness or numbness of satisfaction; and the *fantasy* addictions, which draw pleasure from the escape or stimulation of fantasy. Ironically, addictive searches for power lead into conditions of profound powerlessness,[57] and entrance into recovery from addiction can only be sought by admitting powerlessness. Really, the search in sexual addictions is a search for love, addictively confusing sexual power over someone else with the assurance that one will overcome all the deep-seated feelings of inadequacy and loss of self, and that, finally, one will be loved.[58] A cycle of shame and the compulsive need to flex the muscle of addictive power alternate with each other; the more the addict tries to become powerful, the more he becomes powerless. The only recovery is in admitting powerlessness and acknowledging a higher power.

Addictive behavior operates around certain core beliefs that truly are "diseased thinking." These core beliefs include impaired statements about self, such as, "I am basically a bad, unworthy person," "No one would love me the way I am," "My needs are never going to be met if I have to depend on others," and "Sex is my most important need."[59] Denial prevents reality from encroaching upon the addictive cycle, and so the cycle continues to spiral. Nowhere is this cycle more obvious than in sexual addictions that involve what is called sexual abuse. We can fairly say that all sexually addicted behavior is abusive of someone, either of the victim or of the supposed "victor" in this compulsive power play.[60] Behavior becomes more abusive as boundaries are dissolved in the downward spiraling cycle of shame and denial, and the addict becomes more and more powerless in his desperate attempt to maintain power.[61] Interestingly, rather than the discipline of celibacy inclining someone to sexual addiction, the reverse is true: all sex addicts can profit from the practice of celibacy by gaining some sobriety from sexual "intoxication," since even autoerotic sexual behavior and fantasy inhibits achievement of sexual sobriety.[62]

What is needed in the Church today is a priesthood of servant hearts, unafraid of power yet not intoxicated by it—servant hearts authorized in their priesthood by the servant heart of Jesus Christ. Like Jesus, ordained priests must be meek and humble of heart; they must not be afraid to be consumed in self-gift through the self-gift of Jesus Christ, who has called them to follow Him more closely. As we seek to look more penetratingly into the unchanging heart of the priesthood, let us examine how our human heart has been created in the image and likeness of God's divine heart and reflect upon human love in the divine plan.

The HUMAN HEART *in the* DIVINE PLAN

THE ORIGINAL MEANING
OF SEXUALITY AND BODILINESS

*I*n his already classic biography of Pope John Paul II, Dr. George Weigel refers to the conferences that the pope gave during his Wednesday audiences between 1979 and 1984, which have been collected under the title "theology of the body." Calling these writings a "theological time bomb," Dr. Weigel estimates that it may take almost a century for this teaching to be widely assimilated and appreciated.[1] *The Theology of the Body: Human Love in the Divine Plan* is indeed the most excellent and penetrating analysis of human love and of human sexuality and bodiliness that I have discovered in all the literature of Christian theology and anthropology, as well as in the scientific literature of psychology and psychoanalysis.

In *The Theology of the Body*, Pope John Paul II offers an exegesis of the opening chapters of the Book of Genesis that goes back to the beginning—the very "beginning" to which Jesus points in the Gospels of Saint Matthew and Saint Mark when talking with the Pharisees about the indissolubility of marriage in the divine plan:

> "Have you not read that he who made them from the beginning made them male and female, and said, 'For this reason, a man

shall leave his father and mother and be joined to his wife, and the two shall become one? So they are no longer two but one. What therefore God has joined together, let no man put asunder." They said to him, "Why then did Moses command one to give a certificate of divorce, and to put her away?" He said to them, "For your hardness of heart Moses allowed you to divorce your wives, but from the beginning it was not so." (Mt. 19:4–8; Mk. 10:3–9)

The "beginning" is before the time of history, which began at the creation of man as male and female as the culmination of the seven days of creation: "'Let us make man in our image, after our likeness.'. . . God created man in his own image; in the image of God he created him" (Gen. 1:26–27). This passage indicates "the definition of man on the basis of his relationship with God"; man cannot be reduced to the world, nor can he be understood apart from his origins, from his relationship with God. In a second, older account of creation, found in the second chapter of Genesis (2:5–25) the first man is called 'adam until woman is created from his own body; from there on (Gen. 2:18–23), he is called ish and she is called ishshah. This reflects the man's recognition that she is taken from his own flesh: "This at last is bone of my bones and flesh of my flesh; she shall be called Woman, because she was taken out of Man" (Gen. 2:22–23). Marriage is a return to the original union of man and woman: "Therefore a man leaves his father and his mother and cleaves to his wife, and they become one flesh" (Gen. 2:24).[2]

What exists from the beginning of creation and from the creation of man in God's own image is "original." Adam and Eve possessed *original innocence*, wherein they felt no shame in their nakedness, being outside knowledge of good and evil (Gen. 2:25, 17). This "original" is prehistoric, fundamental to integral human nature before the descent of the Fall into original sin. The original image and likeness of man to God, right from the beginning, constitutes the divine plan in all its originality: "Historical man is, so to speak, rooted in his revealed theological prehistory."[3] Everything about our human historical existence must be understood in reference to that beginning, in reference to our prehistoric original innocence as created in the image and likeness of God, though this was lost through original sin. That is why Jesus referred back to it when He was reminding the Pharisees of the essence of human marriage in light of the meaning of the human heart in the divine plan.

Let us look more closely at our human sexuality from the perspective of this divine plan for created humanity, in the image and likeness of which we can see God reflected.

God created us male and female, and this creation in all its original innocence is *bodily*. As we seek to understand our creation in the image and likeness of God, our bodiliness serves not as an obstacle but as a disclosure of the unique way in which the human person is bodily. We do not simply *have* a body; rather, we *are* bodily and have a relationship with our own body unlike any other creature. Our body is our face, our self-expression, and is intimately part of who we are. In our bodiliness lies the capacity for the most intimate self-revelation and self-sharing.

Indeed, the intimacy between male and female is grounded in the recognition that they are of the same flesh—a recognition of bodiliness originally without shame. Because original sin caused a loss of original innocence, the need for "the redemption of our bodies" now exists (Rom. 8:23), a redemption promised by God from the moment of the original sin. In light of our remarks in the previous chapter, it is important to recognize here the boundaries between God and man that are crossed in sin—such transgressions confuse other boundaries between good and evil, between innocence and sin. The body is in no way evil, nor is sexuality sinful; in their original, created innocence God saw that they were good. But the divine plan was not realized, and what was created good in the beginning became fallen and groans in need of redemption by Christ: "The redemption of the body guarantees the continuity and unity between the hereditary state of man's sin and his original innocence, although this innocence was, historically, lost by him irremediably."[4] This redemption guarantees the original goodness of human bodiliness and sexuality, created according to the plan and in the image and likeness of God, and found by Him to be good.

Let us reflect on our being the image and likeness of God—particularly in our bodies and in our sexuality, and thus in our hearts—and look more closely at the divine plan found in original innocence. Pope John Paul II elaborates on this by speaking also of our original solitude. After creating man (Adam) from the dust from the ground (our bodiliness), and after placing him over all the other creatures of the earth, God recognized that "it is not good that man should be alone; I will make him a helper fit for him" (Gen. 2:18). Pope John Paul emphasizes that this original solitude is not just the solitude of the male who does not yet have his female, but is derived from human nature and a part of the original human condition. The deeper meaning of human solitude, of the aloneness of man, lies deeper than and is prior to the original unity containing the difference between the sexes, and has to do with the uniqueness of man in his original solitude among all other creatures.[5] This is represented in the Book of Genesis by the account of God forming every beast of the field and bird of the air out of the ground, and then bringing them to man to see what he would call them (Gen. 2:19). As Pope John Paul explains:

> Man's subjectivity is already emphasized through this. . . . The first meaning of man's original solitude is defined on the basis of a specific test or examination which man undergoes before God (and in a certain way also before himself). By means of this test, man becomes aware of his own superiority, that is, he cannot be considered on the same footing as any other species of living beings on the earth. . . . Right from the first moment of his existence, created man finds himself before God as if in search of his own entity. It could be said he is in search of the definition of himself. . . . The fact that man "is alone" in the midst of the visible world and, in particular, among living beings, has a negative significance in this search, since it expresses what he "is not.". . . . Nevertheless, the fact of not being able to identify himself essen-

tially with the visible world . . . has, at the same time, a positive aspect. Man finds himself alone before God mainly to express, through a first self-definition, his own self-knowledge.[6]

Original solitude is inherent in human subjectivity, both as self-conscious and self-determining. Thus, being "alone" is part of the ontological structure of our humanity as created in the image of God; it is that which enables me to become a "subject constituted as a person." In this way, man is "manifested as a subject of the covenant" and becomes "a partner of the Absolute," alone before God in his ability to discern between good and evil, between life and death.[7]

Yet man is at the same time, as part of the visible world, a body among bodies, among all the other living beings *(animalia)*, which also makes him aware of being alone, of his original solitude: "On the basis of the experience of his own body . . . he reached the conviction that he was 'alone.'"[8] The meaning of our human bodiliness and of our original solitude is borne out in how only Adam alone, made from the dust of the earth (Gen. 2:7), is capable of tilling the earth and subduing it (Gen. 2:5, 1:28). Our bodiliness makes our subjectivity and self-consciousness concrete and individual, personal and specifically human. Human original solitude places man in his bodiliness before the Creator as alone among His creatures, places him before the tree of knowledge of good and evil. Human bodiliness distinguishes us from all other creatures by placing us before God. The visibleness of the human body before other bodies opens the human heart in opening out what is invisible about our humanity before God: that we stand before the alternative of good and evil, of death and life, in submission to or in rebellion against our total dependence upon God. The two ways of being a body in this same human being created in the image of God are discovered in the joy and exaltation of man awakening from sleep as male and female, with his circle of solitude broken: "The meaning of man's original unity, through masculinity and femininity, is expressed as an overcoming of the frontier of solitude. At the same time it is an affirmation—with regard to both human beings—of everything that constitutes man in solitude. In the Bible narrative, solitude is the way that leads to that unity which, following Vatican II, we can define as *communio personarum*,"[9] or "a communion of persons." Here a transcendence, inherently human as created in the image and likeness of God, is recognizable: an opening toward a reciprocity of a communion of persons in relationship, corresponding to our human capacity for love from the depths of our human heart. Our creation in the image and likeness of God is most penetratingly seen as our creation in the image and likeness of the Trinity: just as God is One and a communion of three Persons, so man is created bodily as one *'adam* in an original unity of the communion of the male and female, *ish* and *ishshah*,[10] who are created as bodily with the capacity to cleave to one another and become one flesh in God (Gen. 2:24). Thus, "the body reveals man": in a bodily, sexual way, male and female discover their own humanity, both in its original unity and in the duality of their mysterious mutual attraction as "he" and "she," as they become one flesh, revealing themselves most personally by becoming of one heart. In this their self-revelation becomes incarnate, expressed most fully in the conjugal act in which they submit their whole humanity and communion of love to the divine blessing of fertility.[11] All this unfolds in the image and likeness of God, who revealed Himself in the Incarnation of His Word, of His beloved Son (Jn. 1:11), the outpouring of God's Trinitarian communion of love.

NUPTIAL LOVE, MARRIED AND CELIBATE

Sexuality is thus a certain "surpassing of the limit of man's solitude that is inherent in the constitution of his body, and determines its original meaning. This surpassing always contains within it a certain assumption of the solitude of the body of the second 'self' as one's own."[12] If conjugal love is a surpassing of the original solitude of man before God in his fundamental constitution as human being, celibacy for the sake of the kingdom and for the sake of entering into an exclusive spousal relationship with Christ intensifies human indwelling in the original solitude of man before God, that original solitude which Pope John Paul calls "the original virginal value of man."[13] This insight can deepen our earlier reflection on the meaning of celibacy in light of loneliness and aloneness, now seen in terms of how this can be lived bodily in priestly celibacy, as a remaining in an original solitude so as to be alone, to be "all one"[14] in participating in the communion of love in the Trinity and in the communion of love in the Church, as a true incarnation of that communion in ordained, ministerial priesthood. We spoke of the grieving involved in letting go of loneliness, and now we can see this as a "letting go," so as to dwell in original solitude for the sake of a different, a celibate participation in the communion of love with God and with the Church— a priestly participation. Can we say that, as conjugal love through mutual choice assumes as one's own the solitude of the body of the second self, so in the acceptance of the vocation of celibacy, a priest assumes as his own the solitude of the body of Christ and offers his own original solitude to Christ and His Body, the Church, in mutual self-donation?

Original nakedness, in which the male and female were naked yet not ashamed (Gen. 2:25), describes their mutual bodily experience of their femininity and masculinity together, each discovering himself or herself with the help of the other, directly through the body, that is, sexually, in the full consciousness of the meaning of the body (Gen. 2:25) before sin. In original sin, the eyes of both are opened (Gen. 3:7), and they awaken from the sleep of the original innocence of their original nakedness into the self-consciousness of conscience awakened, in which they know that they are naked and are ashamed. Shame arises as they now see that they are naked; original nakedness is now experienced on the other side of a boundary crossed by sin. In shame, a human being now experiences fear with regard to the "second self." This experience takes place deep in the heart and also before the other self, fearing for one's own self in the need for affirmation and acceptance by the "second self." In original nakedness there is an original absence of shame: the experience of being originally given to each other fully in an intimacy at once simple and pure, in the fullness of a mutual knowledge of the personal reality and truth of each one. This sharing of the deepest interiority of each in an external perception becomes a common union that is "communion," in the original nakedness of each, as seen by the Creator Himself who saw that it was very good (Gen. 1:31).[15]

Original sin is understood as the loss of original justice; this loss of justice is not merely abstract, however, and must always be understood within the loss of relationship, of communion. The loss of original righteousness arises in the experience of its loss in the knowledge of good and evil, as the crossing of the boundary disturbs the "tranquil testimony of conscience" which "precedes any experience of good and evil."[16] In losing the purity of heart of original innocence, shame disrupts mutual dignity and threatens the personal intimacy that is at the very heart of the meaning of the body and of sexuality, at the very heart of the meaning of communion: the original nuptial meaning of the body from the beginning.[17]

The nuptial meaning of the body is the nuptial meaning of our whole human existence as gift and is the way in which we most fully are in the image of God, capable of making a total gift of ourselves and capable of understanding and becoming an image of the radical gift of creation, through which we have been called into existence out of total nothingness. To be human is to be called to participate in the divine communion of love, in mutual self-giving as a person, body and soul.[18]

This nuptial meaning of the body is an interior freedom from dominance by the sexual instinct, and thus a freedom from shame. This freedom gives the capacity to express love the way the Trinity loves, in which the *person* giving is the *gift*.[19] As Pope Paul VI writes regarding the pastoral constitution *Gaudium et Spes*, "Let us recall here the text of the last Council which declared that man is the only creature in the visible world that God willed 'for its own sake.' It then added that man 'can fully discover his true self only in a sincere giving of himself.'"[20]

The privation of this nuptial meaning of the body is the reduction of the other human being to an "object for me," which can involve an actual extortion of the gift of self from the other person or can simply be any interior reduction of the person to a mere object for my possession.[21] This is the beginning of shame, as I turn the other and turn myself into an object, destroying personal intimacy and communion in the act. Often this objectification is intensely bodily, putting emphasis on the physical and sexual by focusing on the sensual. The emphasis here is on taking, possessing, or at least using. Gone is any sense of free gift given and received in mutual self-discovery and self-disclosure, which can lead to the only real self-possession, the only true single-heartedness, which comes in self-giving. The bodily is seized upon because it is visible and tangible, and the sexual is emphasized in its promise to cross all boundaries to the limitless, exalting myself beyond all limit—which is ultimately a false infinity.

To give oneself genuinely, on the other hand, involves a disinterestedness, an ability to go beyond the purely physical dimension of the body and sex, even in conjugal love: "The human body, oriented interiorly by the sincere gift of the person, reveals not only its masculinity or femininity on the physical plane, but reveals also such a value and such a beauty as to go beyond the purely physical dimension of sexuality."[22] Like the original solitude, the body and sex are not left behind in nuptial love but are surpassed, and lead to the communion of persons.

As all self-gift is nuptial, surely also the self-gift of a celibate person is nuptial; it involves bodiliness and sexuality, both male and female. An angelism of celibacy can mistakenly see the celibate priestly life as no longer having anything to do with the body or with sexuality. This in turn can spawn all the psychological, physical, and spiritual problems that arise out of the dishonesty with self that comes from being out of touch with one's own desires, sexuality, and body.

Pope John Paul II emphasizes the pervasiveness of sexuality and the body in any act of love by any individual person, in his or her irrepeatable uniqueness. It is ironic that Pope John Paul's theology of the body has been criticized as reducing the body to sexuality and presumably understanding sexuality in a way that reduces it to biology, "rather than an emotional and spiritual communication through the body."[23] Strangely, this misunderstanding is the same one often made regarding Freud, and fails to appreciate how John Paul II understood sexuality so pervasively that its mystery can only be comprehended in his expression "nuptial meaning of the body." As he says,

> The nuptial meaning of the body, connected with masculinity-femininity . . . indicates a particular capacity of expressing love, in which man becomes a gift. On the other hand, the capacity and deep availability for the affirmation of the person corresponds to it . . . someone willed by the Creator for his or her own sake . . . someone chosen by eternal Love. The affirmation of the person is nothing but acceptance of the gift, which, by means of reciprocity, creates the communion of persons. . . . The nuptial meaning of the body explains man's original happiness.[24]

While the union between a man and woman, which becomes conjugal and procreative, constitutes the fundamental meaning of the nuptial capacity of the human person, before "becoming husband and wife, the man and the woman emerge from the mystery of creation in the first place as brother and sister in the same humanity. Understanding the nuptial meaning of the body in its masculinity and femininity reveals the depths of the freedom which is the freedom of giving."[25] This allows us to consider *all* human relationships, including those that are not conjugal or are not between persons of the opposite sex. It allows us to consider relationships lived within a celibate priestly ministry. Within the context of his teaching on the nuptial meaning of the body, Pope John Paul identifies the meaning of a vocation to celibacy:

Christ revealed to man and woman, over and above the vocation to marriage, another vocation—namely, that of renouncing marriage, in view of the kingdom of heaven. With this vocation, he highlighted the same truth about the human person. If a man or a woman is capable of making a gift of himself for the kingdom of heaven, this proves in its turn (and perhaps even more) that there is the freedom of the gift in the human body. It means that this body possesses a full nuptial meaning.[26]

Thus celibacy as lived by an ordained priest, or by any person, and every chaste relationship that is truly self-giving, is nuptial in the full sense. We will elaborate on this further in the fifth chapter.

Relationships with persons of the same sex initially serve to consolidate sexual identity so as to make possible deeper relationships with persons of the opposite sex. Yet every self-giving relationship is nuptial, and every relationship is bodily and involves the male and female sexuality of the participants, even when the communion of love in self-gift does not entail the particular reciprocity possible for two people of the opposite sex. Moral, psychological, and spiritual problems arise if the communion of love between two persons of the same sex tries to claim the exclusivity proper to a conjugal bond between persons of the opposite sex, particularly when it seeks some type of physical, genital consummation. But there are many ways in which communion and intimacy are genuinely shared in friendship by individual persons of the same sex, in a genuinely nuptial self-gift, though there is no marriage bond with its corresponding rights and claims. This helps us to understand all celibate love. Since the "body, and it alone, is capable of making visible what is invisible: the spiritual and the divine," the body is involved nuptially in every relationship. Every relationship is "sacramental" in its bodiliness, in that it is "a sign that transmits effectively in the visible world the invisible mystery hidden in God from time immemorial."[27] The union of those in a communion of love can admit of a bodily becoming one without becoming "one flesh," a oneness that is no less real though it does not act out that union or consummate it in a physical, genital way. Such communion of love is available, therefore, in different ways in relationships of the same sex or of the opposite sex.

Accordingly, sexual difference clearly "decides not only the somatic individuality of man, but defines at the same time his personal identity and concreteness."[28] Androgynous longings are evident throughout the history of human civilization and culture, in ways that are complex and ambivalent. Prevalently in our own times there has also been a certain fascination for what is "unisex," for what confuses the boundaries of gender and sexual difference. There are always reasons why an individual or culture is more comfortable with an ambiguity over sexual differences, or, alternately, are disturbed unless gender identity is delineated with perfect clarity and unequivocally defined. While there is a great deal of relativity to how a particular culture or individual at a particular moment incarnates masculinity or femininity into his or her life, there is a particularity and specificity to each of the two sexes; and there is surely something problematic about the need to deny or level the difference and therefore the complementarity between them.

Pope John Paul affirms that the human person "from the beginning, searches for the meaning of his own body. . . . According to Genesis 4:1, the man 'knows' the woman, his wife, for the first time in the act of conjugal union. He is that same man who, by imposing names, that is, also by 'knowing,' differentiated himself from the whole world of living beings or *animalia,* affirming himself as a person and subject." Yet sexual identity and personal identity are more than just "givens" since, whatever "a one-sidedly 'naturalistic' mentality might say about it, in Genesis 4:1 it cannot be a question of passive acceptance of one's own determination by the body and by sex, precisely because it is a question of knowledge." Rather, the discovery of the meaning of one's own body is "a common and reciprocal discovery," made in the most powerful way in the conjugal union between a man and a woman that is procreative: "The woman stands before the man as a mother, the subject of a new human life that is conceived and develops in her, and from her is born into the world. Likewise the mystery of man's masculinity, that is the generative and fatherly meaning of the body, is also thoroughly revealed. . . . Procreation brings it about that the man and woman (his wife) know each other reciprocally in a 'third,' sprung from them both."[29]

The human participation in the communion of love, which is God in the Trinity, cannot be imaged any more vividly than here, where the love and mutual self-gift of the two, the male and the female, begets the new life of a third through the power of God. "I have gotten a man with the help of the Lord" (Gen. 4:1). In the birth of a new human being, the image of God is reproduced and made visible.[30] Thus the communion of love between a man and a woman can become fruitful in a way that uniquely reflects God's creative activity and the mystery of the Incarnation in its redemptive fruitfulness,[31] that is, a way that reflects the perfection of personal difference and communion in the life of the Trinity. Conjugal love between a man and woman most fundamentally and visibly incarnates and participates in the divine life of the Trinity, a love in which celibate priesthood participates in the same yet in a different way.

FALLENNESS AND AFFLICTIONS OF THE HEART

Adam's words to God, "I was afraid, because I was naked; and I hid myself" (Gen. 3:10), lead us from our consideration of the original to an analysis of what is actual in the world as well as in the Church, including afflictions of the priestly heart. Indeed, the original innocence is difficult to even think about, much less look for in our experience of sexuality in our times. Yet it is never completely lost, for if it were, there would be no fear, no haunting desperation, no disquieting yearning. It is in the face of this urgent yearning that solutions are sought which in fact undercut and reduce nuptiality to objectification, the body to sensuality, and sexuality to genitality. These reductions become well-worn paths traversed by media, profane conversation, banter and teasing, and other "innocent" ways of "having fun" and "only being human."

We are speaking of the Fall, the loss of original innocence, the
rupture of the original spiritual and somatic unity,[32] the loss of personal integrity, the entanglement of the nuptiality of the body and
of sexuality in cycles of repetitious behavior, the fear which is never
calmed and even exacerbated in attempts to overpower the object of
love by objectifying it, and the consequent loss of communion. The
tree of life and the knowledge of good and evil promised so much
to the first man and woman; but what happens to good and evil
when life is not received as a gift but is grasped at, when life is made
into an object, an attempt to assume equality with God and the
power and domination of never having to die? Then selfish power
takes the place of love, and life or love that is grasped at inevitably
becomes an object of envy and lust. Lust easily substitutes itself for
love, with which it becomes confused, and the insatiability of lust
aggravates desperation leading to even more objectification. The
impulse to dominate then increases. Pope John Paul especially
expressed concern over how women particularly can become victims
of such domination and abuse.[33] Other weak and vulnerable persons
likewise become victims of distortions of sexuality. Often the
oppressed become the new oppressors, and the cycle goes on.

There is an insatiability to the sexual desire for union and communion, and often the body seems to get the blame when lust has
taken over and shame descends upon us.[34] This can lead to an
obsession with the body, or, alternately, to a massive denial of bodiliness or an inability to live bodily in a healthy manner. In either
extreme, the problem lies in the substitution of objectification for
relationship, leading to all kinds of distortions of bodiliness and
sexuality that depersonalize and threaten the nuptial meaning of the
body. There is an "autogenous force" to the "natural and somatic
substratum of human sexuality" that is coercive and insistent,[35] having an unavoidable urgency that can become compulsive and can
allow sex to become determinative of much of an individual's functioning and life, particularly in sexual addictions, as we have seen.[36]

The religious meaning of sexuality and bodiliness is inherent in
their nuptiality. At the same time, distortions can distort religious

meaning as well, and it should be no surprise that some of the same fallen tendencies regarding the divine plan can be found among members of the Body of Christ, the Church, and certainly also within her leadership and among those who are supposed to be somehow "set apart" with regard to sexuality and desire. Religious taboos regarding sexuality are common; under the Old Law there was a certain sense that sexuality was impure, particularly in association with idolatry.[37] At the same time, the Wisdom literature, and later the Prophets, such as Hosea, Isaiah, and Ezekiel, often represent God as a spouse and speak of Israel as nuptially united with Him despite Israel's unfaithfulness, her adultery. Indeed, throughout the history of Israel up to the very time of Jesus it is adultery that is singled out as the extreme sexual sin, as the sin against the body and against nuptial love (Ezek. 16:5–8, 12–15, 30–32).[38] Under the New Law, Christ extends this bodily sin to the heart, noting that adultery can already be committed there (Mt. 5:27–28) and that, beyond observing monogamy, it is the desire in the heart that determines whether sin has destroyed the human dignity of the other by turning her or him into an object of lust. Thus, as Pope John Paul points out, mutual attraction differs from lust: in this sense two people who are *not* married can experience a mutual attraction for each other which is in no way sinful, yet it is just as certainly possible for two people who *are* married to sin by looking at each other with lust.[39] In plumbing the depths of our humanity, we can identify in the analyses of the "masters of suspicion"—Sigmund Freud, Friedrich Nietzsche, and Karl Marx—three forms of lust: in "the Nietzschean interpretation, the judgement and accusation of the human heart correspond in a way to what is called in biblical language 'the pride of life'; in the Marxist interpretation, to what is called 'the lust of the eyes'; in the Freudian interpretation, to what is called 'the lust of the flesh.'"[40] Lust can arise out of desire, as can love. As Saint Thomas Aquinas realized, the passions are what are transformed into virtue, though they can lead to sin. Desire and its attractions, which are by no means sinful in themselves, can be

a source of enjoyment which leads to praise and celebration of the
beauty of bodiliness; it can potentiate nuptiality.

Pope John Paul goes on to suggest that in this sense the nuptial
meaning of the body is "the antithesis of Freudian libido," as the
meaning of life and of the whole of existence containing the nuptial meaning of the body is "the antithesis of the interpretation of
suspicion" by which the human heart would always need to be
regarded with suspicion. It is true that Freud discussed "love" in
terms of "idealized cathexis" in "object relations." In many ways,
Freud failed to distinguish adequately between relationship and
objectification of the other person. He certainly remained cynical
about love, calling it a neurosis, and believed that altruism and love
of neighbor cover over self-seeking libido. In these ways he always
remained suspicious of love and suspicious of religion. For Freud,
eros, the fundamental impetus to form higher unities, is always in
tension with *thanatos,* the impetus to break down higher unities
into earlier inanimate forms in death.[41] Pope John Paul's theology
of the body, on the other hand, sets out "to define the relationship
of the enunciation of the Sermon on the Mount (Mt. 5:17–18)
with the wide sphere of erotic phenomena." This would include all
that is meant by Freudian libido and more, including all that the
body and sexuality bring to our humanity as Freud saw them, but,
recognizing the need for the "redemption of the body," seeing "the
necessity of overcoming what is derived from lust in its three forms.
. . . It is necessary to rediscover continually in what is erotic the
nuptial meaning of the body and the true dignity of the gift . . .
which means that the aspiration of the human spirit toward what
is true, good and beautiful" expands "so that what is erotic also
becomes true, good and beautiful."[42]

FROM THE ORIGINAL TO THE ACTUAL

Pope John Paul's theology of the body carefully distinguishes
"desire pure and simple" from "sexual desire . . . linked with noble
gratification" and points out the need for honesty. He calls for a
"spontaneity" of heart which does not need to be suspicious, but

can enjoy the spontaneity that "is the gradual fruit of the discernment of the impulses of one's own heart."[43] Richard Sipe, referring specifically to the maturity needed to live celibacy in a healthy way, observes that "People who do not know their desires—that is, their innermost self—cannot 'grow up,'" and emphasizes the importance of knowing "our sexuality by paying attention to our desires, the implications of our gender, the degree of our sexual drive, the objects of our sexual excitation, our sexual orientation." For otherwise, one aspiring to live a celibate life in fact "consolidates personality at an adolescent level of psychosexual integration," which "restricts them" so that they "are condemned to rely on impulsive sexual play or occasional experimentation alternating with guilt, remorse, and abstinence without any real insight into the essence of their desires."[44] Indeed, this type of self-knowledge, while never exhaustively achieved, is necessary to ground not only the possibility of celibacy but of all perseverance and constancy from within, from the heart. "Staying with our desire" does not mean experimentation or allowing oneself to sin. Rather, prayer is the place for us to stay with our desires, bringing all our contradictions, ambivalences, and strivings of our heart and mind before God, seeing these in His light and allowing His light to illuminate every relationship and everything we do. Rather than flirting with an occasion of sin, this requires an "asceticism" which is necessary for growth to sexual maturity, just as restraint or emotional asceticism is necessary in the pursuit of self-knowledge through any process of spiritual direction or the psychoanalytic process: "The great paradox, that both sexual deprivation and sexual activity can lead to radical self knowledge, is resolved in the crucible of love. Quite simply, we know our heart of hearts by acknowledging who and what we desire. Further self-knowledge is hammered out in relationships. Desire is refined by the truth of our loves and the fulfillment of our duty to others."[45] This is the good old-fashioned "self-control" that makes possible continence, the mastery and temperance of desires, abstinence, and chastity, all grounded and integrated in ways that potentiate rather than restrict the deepest freedom of the human person for love in nuptial self-gift, which alone can ground faithfulness and commitment.[46]

Failure to know and to stay with our desires not only arrests spiritual development; it can also lead to serious sexual patholo- gy, sexual "acting out," and sexual abuse. In the next chapter, we will consider the afflicted priestly heart in terms of sexuality. Much sexual knowledge and openness to sexual desire and experi- ence seem to characterize our contemporary world, yet in a way that hardly seems to be furthering our human or spiritual growth and maturity. What can we understand by comparing levels of human and sexual maturity and commitment among celibate priests with that of their contemporaries, married and single?[47]

Some overall trends may help to set the stage. In America, we live in a society where "about half the teenagers of various racial and ethnic groups in the nation have begun having intercourse with a partner in the age range of fifteen to eighteen, and at least four out of five have had intercourse by the time their teenage years are over."[48] This gives us some sense of the climate in which the Church's advocacy of abstinence needs to be heard, though more recent studies have discerned a decrease in sexual activity among teenagers. The AIDS scare has surely made a contribution to this decrease, but there is an interesting increase in the number of men who are still virgins at age twenty, though there has not been a parallel increase in the number of women who maintain their virginity until that age.[49] To understand these trends and their implications, the researchers of the study *Sex in America* offer several classifications of sexual attitudes: those who are *traditional,* always guided by religious beliefs and tending to reject homosex- uality, legalized abortion, and premarital, teenage, and extramari- tal sex; those who are *relational,* believing that sex should always be part of a loving relationship, though it need not always be reserved for marriage; and those whose sexual attitudes are *recre- ational,* viewing sex as something that does not necessarily have anything to do with love. In the research cited here, the members of the traditional group constituted about one-third of those sampled, the relational about one-half of those surveyed, and the recreational a little more than a quarter of the sample population.[50] While the relational group has subsets which include "religious," "conventional," and "contemporary religious," in this survey religion is still predominantly associated with the traditional attitudes—which leaves me uncomfortably wondering whether we are still locked in stereotypes of "religion" that may influence our eventual conclusions about attitudes. It is interesting to see that, according to this research, Catholic men tend to be 17.8 percent traditional, 49.6 percent relational, and 32.6 percent recreational in their attitudes toward sexuality, while Catholic women are 22.2 percent traditional, 58 percent relational, and only 19.8 percent recreational in their sexual attitudes.[51]

With regard to stereotypes and preconceptions, we must readily admit that religion, and certainly faith in Christ, brings with it convictions that do indeed affect our attitudes toward sexuality and its deepest meaning. It can be very difficult, therefore, for priestly celibacy to be comprehensible outside that faith attitude. With regard to priesthood and sexuality, and considering their meaning in reference to a celibate commitment, we might start off with the assessment of Richard Sipe, who clearly has researched carefully yet has proposed the shocking and rather confusing estimate based on "more than thirty years of research" that "at any one time at least 50 percent of priests, all of whom are bound by the law of celibacy and publicly claim the identity 'celibate,' are in fact practicing celibacy."[52] When reported in the media at the time he first made this assertion, it had the effect of a devastating exposé of rampant infidelity on the part of one out of two priests. It seems that Sipe wants to have the opposite impact, for he insists that he finds it "quite a remarkable assertion if one reflects on its implications," that at least half of those who by law and identity profess celibacy would "in reality" be "actively involved in the process of celibate achievement, by intention and behavior, free from gross rationalization, denial, or psychologically splitting their sexual energies." Moreover, Sipe seems to define the practice of celibacy rather modestly, as not even falling into "one or two lapses in the course of a year."[53]

Richard Sipe does seem very sincere in his high esteem of those who live a celibate commitment: "In my early development, I do not think I made a mistake trusting priests and nuns, turning to them because I revered their celibate dedication. I have found that priests and nuns who achieve celibacy are an awesome lot. They manifest an interior freedom, an integration that unites their individuality with their service. Their spirituality is marked by their efforts and their achievements. We all have a great deal to learn from them."[54] Nonetheless, this praise notwithstanding, the impact of his "50 percent estimate" seems to have eroded confidence in the overall commitment of those publicly professing celibacy, and even after trying to understand the force of what he really wants to say, his estimation that one out of two priests is sexually active in the sense of being sexually involved with another person, though professing celibacy, is not very edifying. Even if the other 50 percent of those publicly professing celibacy are not sexually active, this is rather disappointing and not a very impressive scenario in comparison with the commitment of those who publicly profess a marital commitment since, according to one study, 80 percent of women and 65 to 85 percent of men report that they had no other partners than their spouse while married.[55]

According to that same study, those who actually undertake a public marital commitment are those more likely to be "traditional" rather than "recreational" in their approach to sexuality; while 94 percent of married people report having only one sexual partner in the past year, 75 percent of those never married but living together and 80 percent of those married before but now living with someone indicate the same degree of fidelity. According to the same survey, those who are more educated are more likely to have a recreational rather than a traditional view of sexuality and are more likely to have had more sexual partners over a lifetime.[56] Statistics on trends for divorce show that the chance of being divorced by the tenth wedding anniversary was about one in five for those married between 1933 and 1942, but escalates to one in three for those couples married between 1943 and 1952, and to a 38 percent chance for those couples married between 1953 and 1962.[57] One cannot avoid the conclusion that maintaining commitment has to do with living that commitment as fully and radically as possible. Thus, the *Times Review* of La Crosse, Wisconsin, on February 15, 2001, reported that while only 50 percent of those Catholics married by a justice of the peace persevered in their marriage, 67 percent of those who married in the Church persevered. The odds of a successful marriage get even better when couples use natural family planning, with such couples having a divorce rate of only 3.5 percent; when they also attend Mass together there is only a 2 percent divorce rate; and when they also pray together only .09 percent divorce rate. One can easily imagine the lower defection rates from celibacy and the priesthood for priests who celebrate Mass, pray the Divine Office, make a holy hour, do spiritual reading on a daily basis, and see a spiritual director regularly.

While speaking of defections from commitments in the priesthood, it is relatively unpublicized that an astonishingly high number of those who have left the priesthood for various reasons have returned. In response to an inquiry by the *National Catholic Register*, "the Vatican's Congregation for the Clergy reported that 9,551 priests who left the ministry between 1968 and 1997 worldwide eventually returned to priestly life. They represent almost 20 percent of the 53,151 diocesan and religious order priests who abandoned their vocation during that period. In the years 1968–78, a world average of 3,152 priests left the ministry per year. The rate dropped to 1,152 per year in the years 1978–97. And the rate of return by priests has been increasing. When Pope John Paul II became pope in 1978, an average of 31.3 men a year were returning. In the 22 years since his election, the average has risen to 396 per year."[58] These high statistics do not include others who may have wished to return to the priesthood but who were unable to do so because they had been validly married in the

Church or had incurred marital and family responsibilities.[59] Moreover, the "total number of diocesan priests in the universal Church—263,521 as of 1997—is almost back to the 1968 level of 269,607, thanks to rapid Third World growth. And the trend in Western countries in recent years has been one of slight but steady growth."[60] While it is difficult to know the true picture regarding the morality and integrity of sexuality among priests and seminarians, it does seem clear that more sexual knowledge and experience is no longer the biggest problem. As in society in general, the problem is a "recreational" attitude toward sexuality. To lift the obligation of celibacy or to liberalize attitudes toward sexuality likewise would fail to solve the problems, as can be seen in the broader society. What is clear is that among married persons as well as among those committed to celibacy those practices and attitudes labeled as "religious" and "traditional" strengthen and preserve marriage and priestly commitment.

If priestly formation and priestly life tended to cut sexuality off from healthy integration, this no longer need be so. Priests must integrate their human sexuality within their relationship with their Lord. The most powerful means of integration is prayer, and, as Archbishop Timothy Dolan has asked, "Why are we embarrassed to take our sexuality to prayer? Why are we afraid to admit our weaknesses, own up to our falls, and ask his grace? Is chastity and celibacy a gift? Well, then, ask for it in prayer! Father Dominic Maruca says, 'You are committing psychic suicide if you think you can be genuinely celibate without a strong ongoing relationship with the Lord.'"[61]

CHAPTER FOUR

The AFFLICTED PRIESTLY HEART

Sexual Misconduct and Homosexuality

CRISIS AND SCANDAL

The beginning of the new millennium saw an explosion of allegations of sexual misconduct against priests and bishops, leaving many enraged at the "cover-up" that allowed such misbehavior to continue. The realization of the extent of sexual misconduct has initially had a paralyzing effect, but as the Church and society continue on the long road of self-examination to change, it is nonetheless essential to try to find some context within which to understand what has happened and what must be done. Exposure in the media has done the service of forcing an honest admission of the reality and scope of the problem, and for this the Church must be grateful. Yet at the same time there seem to have been a number of agendas served in the process of uncovering and analyzing this problem in the Church. The distinction between "allegation" and "conviction" has often been lost in media reports. Newspapers often cover the same incident repeatedly, each time reporting it as if for the first time. And although allegations against individual priests may surface quickly, when accused priests are cleared there is often no report. Strangely, similar misconduct among ministers of other denominations and sectors of society, such as in the public school system, are either not reported or are mentioned on the back page.

Another distinction often blurred is that between true pedophilia and other types of sexual misconduct, leaving the impression
that this is solely a Catholic and priestly problem. Accordingly,
celibacy is often blamed, as is the overall attitude of Catholic sexual morality, which increasingly seems to be a lone voice, alien in
present-day society. Professor Philip Jenkins, author of the definitive study *Pedophiles and Priests: Anatomy of a Contemporary Crisis,*
points out that there is no inherent cause-and-effect relationship
between celibacy and sexual misconduct or abuse: "My research of
cases over the past twenty years indicates no evidence whatever that
Catholic or other celibate clergy are any more likely to be involved
in misconduct or abuse than any denomination—or indeed, than
non-clergy. However determined news media may be to see this
affair as a crisis of celibacy, the charge is just unsupported. Literally
every denomination and faith tradition has its share of abuse cases,
and some of the worst involve non-Catholics."[1]

However, such comparisons are impossible to substantiate
because no other religious denomination has the hierarchical
organization that allows a thorough investigation or that leaves
the paper trail the Catholic Church does. My own clinical psychoanalytic experience over more than twenty years has convinced
me that most pedophilia and sexual abuse of minors is incestuous,
that is, that it takes place within the immediate family.

Why the focus, then, on the Catholic priesthood? I am convinced that the Catholic Church is suffering persecution for,
among other reasons, the clear teaching it has presented in defense
of human life at the United Nations Conferences in Cairo and
Beijing, and for the outspoken criticism of the contemporary
culture of death that it has consistently voiced. Even faithful
Catholics have become so ashamed at the extent of priestly sexual
misconduct, and so infuriated at the failure of Church leadership
to respond to the victims, that many have been silent and blind to
the way this sorry reality has been exploited by the media, as it
seeks to weaken the teaching voice and witness of the Catholic
Church. Dissenting Catholics (if they can even be called Catholic

anymore) have feasted on the scandal as a way to repeatedly demand changes in the Church that would further their own agenda regarding changes in Church teaching and in the very shape of the Church.[2] Some clearly want to destroy the Church. With regard to priesthood, these changes would at least involve changing the discipline of celibacy, if not ordaining married men and women or dismantling the hierarchical structure of the Church or the priesthood altogether.

At a meeting in Dallas in June 2002, the United States Conference of Catholic Bishops (USCCB) adopted the Charter for the Protection of Children and Young People. Ultimately revised in consultation with the Vatican, this charter calls for the formation of outreach programs to assist the victims of sexual abuse in every diocese. It also institutes national and diocesan review boards that are composed primarily of laypersons to aid the investigations of abuse and advise the bishops on appropriate action. These review boards also ensure the removal of any priest from active ministry during the investigation of any serious allegation, as well as the permanent removal and possible laicization of any priest who is found guilty of sexual abuse.[3] By the time the bishops approved the charter, no serious or strong protest was possible against the characterization of this as a "Catholic" and a "priestly" problem or against the discriminatory focus on cases of Catholic priestly and episcopal sexual misconduct, which virtually ignored cases of sexual abuse in other denominations or among other groups who work with children. Practically lost in a barrage of reports on the Dallas bishops' meeting was an article in *Education Week* which, after searching only newspaper archives and not personnel files, found 244 cases in a six-month period of teacher-student sex cases involving allegations of sexual abuse, ranging from unwanted touching to sexual relationships and serial rape.[4] No strong voice protested such discrimination during this frenzy. The Catholic Church (and no other denomination) was coerced to account for how each case was handled, surrender all its confidential personnel files, present its sexual misconduct policy, and provide statistics on allegations against priests dating back four decades. What if the American public school system had been required to do the same?

PEDOPHILIA VERSUS EPHEBOPHILIA

A number of distinctions have been repeatedly asserted during this crisis, though the frenzy has not permitted their implications to sink in. In the first place, most bishops and religious superiors who have over the decades transferred priests to other assignments, perhaps after some treatment or spiritual retreat, were usually responding to the problem as it was understood at the time even by mental health professionals,[5] whose advice was also followed in roughly the same way by school boards and police departments. Unfortunately, even after an awareness of the unique nature of pedophilia and sexual addiction had become evident, some bishops and religious superiors failed to respond adequately and in many cases failed even to remove even serial predators.

Secondly, with such a frighteningly high number of allegations made against priests, it must be remembered that such sexual misconduct seldom involves true pedophilia, that is, sexual abuse of prepubescent children. The term *pedophilia* is usually mistakenly used to name sexual abuse of a minor by someone over the age of eighteen. In fact, pedophilia refers to sexual involvement between an adult and a prepubescent child, while *ephebophilia* refers to sexual involvement of an adult with a pubescent child under the age of eighteen. A causal relationship with celibacy is unlikely since research shows that interactions involving pedophilia are most often of primarily heterosexual orientation;[6] most of those perpetrated by priests are homosexual. Father Stephen Rossetti's experience at Saint Luke's Institute revealed that only one out of four or five priests in treatment for abusing minors had abused prepubescent children—a statistic that is also significant in view of the fact that the prognosis and response to treatment is much more optimistic for ephebophiles, who have only been involved with postpubescent children.[7]

Moreover, most priests who have been engaged in sexual relationships with minors do not display addictive behavior with a series of victims, indicating a better prognosis. Dr. George Abel, who has developed a technique for screening those who might be more vulnerable to becoming abusers of children, found that 377 non-incarcerated child molesters who victimized children outside the home had an average of 72.12 victims and an average of 128.11 acts of abuse, whereas a Saint Luke's Institute sample of 84 priest child molesters had an average of 8.52 victims and an average of 32.14 total sexual contacts.[8] Moreover, follow-up on priests treated at St. Luke's indicates that a priest who has committed sexual abuse, when successfully treated through a continuing program of recovery, is no more likely to relapse than a priest who has never abused a child is likely to start doing so.[9] In the present climate, however, these distinctions are often ignored. In the treatment of this issue, language is black and white, demands are absolute, and reassurances are expected to be absolute guarantees. There is no tolerance for distinctions that are crucial: distinctions between serial predators and those who slipped once, perhaps under the influence of alcohol, stress, or other pressure; between those who looked and those who touched; between those who abused children and those who abused adolescents.

HOMOSEXUAL MISCONDUCT
Repressed or "Stunted" Homosexuality?

A 2004 study by the John Jay College of Criminal Justice, commissioned by the USCCB, would seem to confirm that the incidence of pedophilia among Catholic priests is no higher than among the general population. At the same time, the allegations that are surfacing provide plenty of evidence that there has been a considerable amount of sexual misconduct on the part of Catholic priests, and that much of it has been homosexual.[10] In fact, 80 percent of the allegations against priests audited in the John Jay study involved homosexual behavior—a percentage clearly much higher than in the general population of males.[11] The reasons for such a significant occurrence of sexual misconduct among priests and breakdown of clerical discipline are complex. Yet, once again, context is important, and as Pope John Paul said in April 2002 to the United States cardinals, it is becoming more and more clear that the far-reaching causes of this affliction in the clergy are certainly reflected in the breakdown among married men and women in our society, who probably violate their vows even more frequently than priests do their promise of celibacy.

Surely, seminaries, theology faculties, and Church bureaucracy all bear some of the blame for not screening out unsuitable candidates or for tolerating sexual misconduct among seminarians and priests. But one question still remains: does the priesthood attract men with homosexual tendencies because of its celibacy requirement?

Father Stephen Rossetti, president of St. Luke's Institute, points out that most victims and sexual partners of priests are young males. He notes that a significant number of these priests (not all) are homosexually oriented in a very particular way: they show symptoms of a "regressed" or "stunted" homosexuality, in which they are stuck in adolescence. In most cases, this is in apparent reenactment of molestation they themselves experienced as adolescents.[12] This unfortunately does mean that such developmentally arrested individuals could, if given a particularly conducive climate in seminary or within the presbyterate, feel rather comfortable pursuing a priestly vocation. Given decadent or deficient formation and dissent from moral teaching on sexuality, a permissive atmosphere could thereby incline these individuals toward homosexual "acting out." Such an atmosphere in the seminary and in the priesthood could spread, ultimately driving away healthier men.[13]

As all this becomes more and more clear, undoubtedly there will be some serious scrutiny of these issues of homosexuality in the priesthood, similar to that which has taken place regarding pedophilia. The media and dissenting Catholics, both of which have faulted the bishops and Church leadership for not actively addressing problems of child abuse, will now likely criticize the

Church for acting in a way that is "homophobic" and discriminatory of those of homosexual orientation. But what is most interesting is that the very profile of "stunted homosexuality," which Father Rossetti says characterizes most priests who abuse young males, is precisely the homosexual profile that seems most amenable to treatment and change through a process of integration.[14]

In an open letter to the bishops, the Catholic Medical Association (CMA) of the United States and Canada addressed the phenomenon of "same-sex attraction" (SSA), seeing the problem as one of a denial of sin and a lifetime of loneliness starting in childhood.[15] Often, the problem starts from deficits in the father-son relationship, and can then continue in peer relationships, exhibiting itself in such symptoms as a lack of male confidence, poor body image, sadness, and anger. This can lead to angry rejection of all paternal authority, including the restraints of sexual morality, and to the use and abuse of other males, including adolescents and children. Insisting that no conclusive scientific evidence exists that homosexuality is genetically inherited and cannot be changed, the CMA asserts that even instances of Gender Identity Disorder (GID), along with extreme effeminacy, are amenable to therapeutic intervention, which achieves a bonding between father and son through family therapy, thus affirming the son's masculinity. Distant fathers and overdependence on mothers are often causes of male inadequacy and loneliness, which can lead to homosexual attractions. Recognizing many different causes of SSA, the CMA clearly sees the matter as a correctable developmental arrest. Full recovery is possible through sustained Catholic sexual moral teaching and by fostering a healthy relationship with father figures—the most important of which is a loving relationship with God the Father.

The CMA goes on to observe that some SSA is found in cases of borderline personality disorders, especially those with narcissistic features. These disorders can lead to other problems of substance abuse, sexual paraphilias (perversions), and sexual addiction, with a greater likelihood of having experienced childhood sexual abuse

(40 percent among homosexuals as compared to 16 percent in the general male population). Thus, it does seem to me to be presumptuous to dismiss any connection between SSA and ephebophilia or even pedophilia. Moreover, the intensely narcissistic features of SSA and other above-mentioned pathology is a concern. It would seem, as the CMA notes, that forgiveness is necessary for healing old wounds, and I would add is the only hope of undercutting otherwise unchecked narcissism. The healing of narcissistic wounds through forgiveness allows some dissipation of denial of the truth about homosexuality—an acknowledgement that goes beyond merely seeking acceptance of it, which I have found to be essential to any true integration of homosexuality.

How is such integration possible, and how does this question affect the screening of candidates for the priesthood who experience some homosexual feelings (perhaps even predominantly) so that we do not resort to absolutes in establishing policies? The tendency to act out one's sexual feelings, homosexual or heterosexual, comes from inadequate integration of sexuality, which can be aggravated by other tendencies to impulsivity and addiction, and perhaps even further aggravated by substance abuse and other stressors. This is the complex picture that must be assessed in each candidate for the priesthood: the potential for addiction and impulsivity, and most especially the degree of actual or potential integration of sexuality into a well-consolidated, masculine sexual identity. Yet it is extremely important to realize that it is impossible to integrate homosexuality if it is seen as an option alongside heterosexuality. An individual who experiences predominantly homosexual attractions will only successfully achieve some integration of his sexual orientation *if he recognizes heterosexuality as the norm.*

This certainly goes against the grain of many attitudes in society and even among the psychiatric, psychoanalytic, and psychological establishments. In 1973, no longer considering homosexuality as a "mental disorder," but only a "normal variation of sexual expression," the American Psychiatric Association (APA) deleted homosexuality from its official list of psychiatric disorders in the

Diagnostic and Statistical Manual of Mental Disorders (commonly known as DSM). Defending this move, the APA pointed out that "if one uses the criteria of 'distress' or 'disability,' homosexuality per se is not a mental disorder. If one uses the criterion of 'inherent disadvantage,' it is not at all clear that homosexuality is a disadvantage."[16] Interestingly, a survey conducted the following year indicated that a significant minority of the membership of the APA did not accept this revision of the DSM. Dr. Irving Bieber, a psychoanalyst famous for his contributions to the understanding of homosexuality, objected that, while not a disease or mental disorder, homosexuality should perhaps still be called a "heterosexual dysfunction or inadequacy since it is a developmental abnormality."[17] Nonetheless, while these revisions yet stand in need of support by clinical experience and corresponding theoretical substantiation,[18] psychiatric, psychological, and psychoanalytic manuals and practices have come to reflect an attitude that no longer views homosexuality as pathology but as being compatible with a healthy and normal psychic life.

An item in the final quarterly newsletter of the American Psychoanalytic Association, sent to members in 2000, discusses a talk given by Susan C. Vaughan, former co-chair of the Committee on Gay and Lesbian Issues of the American Psychoanalytic Association, to the Cleveland Psychoanalytic Society and the Association for Psychoanalytic Thought. Speaking from "her determination as a psychoanalyst, clinician, researcher, author, lesbian, and mother," Dr. Vaughan noted "the tremendous changes within the American Psychoanalytic Association [which in] the past decade . . . has changed from an organization that supported 'reparative therapy,' with the intent of changing homosexuals to heterosexuals, to one that accepts homosexual therapists as candidates for analytic training, endorses same-sex marriage, and takes the position that reparative therapy is unlikely to be effective and can hurt people." Vaughan also adds that "there are now about fifty openly gay or lesbian candidates [training to become psychoanalysts] in this country, reminding all analysts that we know less about sexual orientation than we thought we knew."[19]

So much dismissal of what "we thought we knew" sometimes reverts to mere acceptance of one's sexual preference as a simple either/or or as a given, either constitutionally or environmentally. Sexual orientation can probably be best understood in terms of what attraction is predominant; but attractions are complex, and one attraction can cover another as a way of avoiding or defending against another attraction.[20] Recognizing the complexity of sexual attraction can allow us to understand orientation or preference not through labels like "gay" or "straight" but in terms of which is predominant and which is subordinate.[21] In turn, we can then better understand the task of integrating what has been developmentally stunted or cut off and sometimes masked by another attraction. This stunting may involve an inversion, turning back upon earlier stages of development and in upon oneself. It can fixate a homosexual at a point where he is caught between wanting to love another and needing to always find himself in the one he loves, getting entangled over and over again in strategies to love himself. While Heinz Kohut and the "Self Psychologists" later showed this narcissistic tendency to make the one I love a "self object" as pervasive throughout many different psychological strategies besides homosexuality,[22] Freud himself recognized narcissism as a significant factor in homosexuality. There is healthy narcissism, but narcissism that unconsciously never lets go of the loss of being the absolute self is always losing a sense of self and, consequently, always trying to find it.[23]

THE PROCESS OF INTEGRATION

While speaking of sexual orientation in terms of predominant preference, we recognize that the vast majority of individuals have so strong a heterosexual preference that they are virtually unaware of homosexual feelings, integrating these into a normal sexual life. Even for those who experience predominantly same-sex attractions (as with many other people who suffer from some inhibition of ordinary functioning and life in one area), there are often compensatory strengths in other areas and an overall normal healthiness. Therefore, what kind of change are we looking for in order to better integrate homosexuality, and does this involve a "change of orientation"? Must a candidate for ordination to the priesthood attempt to change his sexual orientation, and does God's law call for this?

Though there is nothing sinful about the condition of being predominantly attracted to persons of the same sex, but only in acting upon such attractions in a physical, genital way, a homosexual orientation is a "disordered" affection, a spiritual dysfunction that must be dealt with. Even in the absence of any explicit teaching of Jesus on the matter, the teaching of the *Catechism of the Catholic Church* is well grounded in Sacred Scripture, which unanimously rejects homosexual behavior in both the Old and New Testaments.[24] Every baptized Christian is called to chastity and to refrain from sexual relations outside of marriage. Yet is someone attracted to persons of the same sex, in addition to abstinence from sexual relations, expected to try to change?

Often, the distinction is drawn between *ego-dystonic* homosexuality, which is distressing to the individual, and *ego-syntonic* homosexuality, which causes no particular disadvantage or disability. Freud's point of view on the way in which homosexuality could be treated is very instructive. In a letter to which we already referred, Freud wrote as follows to an American mother who was distraught over the apparent homosexual orientation of her son:

> By asking me if I can help, you mean, I suppose, if I can abolish homosexuality and make normal heterosexuality take its place. The answer is, in a general way, we cannot promise to achieve it. In a certain number of cases we succeed in developing the blighted germs of heterosexual tendencies which are present in every homosexual, in the majority of cases it is no more possible. . . . What analysis can do for your son runs in a different line. If he is unhappy, neurotic, torn by conflicts, inhibited in his social life,

analysis may bring him harmony, peace of mind, full efficiency, whether he remains a homosexual or gets changed.[25]

Nonetheless, Freud remained fundamentally pessimistic about the possibility of converting a homosexual orientation into a heterosexual one, commenting (I suppose wryly) that there was about as much chance of success in doing this as in attempting the conversion in the other direction.[26] Psychoanalysis is both a therapeutic technique and a method of investigation into the unconscious dynamics of the human psyche, and psychoanalysts have always been more confident in the ability of psychoanalysis to penetrate into the psychodynamics of homosexuality than to effect a change in sexual orientation.[27] Many of those who are pessimistic about undertaking such a conversion base their attitude, as did Freud, on convictions about constitutional and biological foundations of a homosexual orientation as much as upon their clinical experience. With respect to actual therapy and clinical work, as Freud already observed, the motivation to change often is lacking: "The homosexual is not able to give up the object of his pleasure, and one cannot convince him that if he changed to the other object he would again find the pleasure he has renounced."[28]

In our own times, there is a chorus of voices (on both sides of the choir) regarding this question; some warn against even taking up the task, while others warn against the moral consequences of not pursuing such a change in sexual orientation as far as possible. In 1990, the American Psychological Association went so far as to adopt a policy stating that "scientific evidence does not show that conversion therapy works" and that it can do more harm than good.[29] When one reviews the strong claims of those who have attempted such therapy to have evidence of overwhelming success, one at least is inclined to keep an open mind on the matter and is left wondering from where within the American Psychological Association the initiative came for such a definitive statement against the attempt.

It is interesting to note that those who argue in favor of reparative therapy for homosexuals continue to rely heavily on some of

the basic insights into the dynamics of parental relationships analyzed by Freud and classical psychoanalytic theory of homosexuality, such as the distant father and the engulfing mother.
Psychoanalysts such as Irving Bieber and Ismond Rosen have sub-
stantiated the importance of the father-son relationship. Many, like
Dr. Joseph Nicolosi, define homosexuality as a reparative drive,
repairing deficits in the original love relationships by forming
relationships in the present with other men and women within
the male/female polarity, in an attempt to get beyond the mirror
narcissism of homosexual infatuation.[30] Dr. Nicolosi does not so
much speak of a therapeutic cure of homosexuality, but of a
change.[31] Dr. Gerard J. M. van den Aardweg highlights that
homosexual dependence on the mother and indifference toward
the father traps the individual in an adolescent ego-centered
thinking and feeling, and he prescribes a therapy like that used
for addictions.[32] The therapeutic approaches for this "same-sex
attachment disorder" are often eclectic, such as the method of
healing proposed by Richard Cohen, who combines behavioral,
cognitive, and psychodynamic therapy to heal wounds that are
not in the first place homosexual or homoerotic, but "homoemo-
tional" or also "heteroemotional"—wounds having to do with
emotions of attachment and loss before they come to be eroti-
cized or sexualized.[33]

Many of these reparative therapies for homosexuality are
strongly based on Christian beliefs or on the Catholic faith.[34] The
Catholic support group Courage seeks to bring together in a
spiritually based fellowship those with same-sex attractions who
are seeking to live chaste lives. Its members dedicate themselves to
Jesus Christ in lives of service, prayer, spiritual direction and
reading, and by frequenting Mass and the sacraments.[35] Salesian
Father John Harvey, the founder, recommends several other support groups allied to the philosophy of Courage, such as chapters
of Exodus International, which integrates Scripture and psychological theory in a supportive approach to healing,[36] and secular
groups such as Sexaholics Anonymous (SA), and Sex and Love

Addicts Anonymous (SLAA). He does not recommend, however, the so-called reformed groups of SA, nor the purportedly Catholic group Dignity, since these last two do not espouse a philosophy of sexual abstinence that conforms to Church teaching.[37]

Father Harvey draws upon the work of therapists such as Dr. Elizabeth Moberly, who even entitles her consideration of homosexuality "a new Christian ethic," prescribing prayer and love as the most necessary elements for the Christian to find healing from homosexual attachments.[38] As have most others who are positive about the treatment of homosexuality, Dr. Moberly prefers the name "same-sex ambivalence" and asserts that it is caused neither by biological or learning deficits but by a disruption in the early years of attachment to the parent of the same sex. The homosexual drive must therefore be understood as an abnormal "disidentification with the parent of the same sex," which is at the same time a drive to repair that deficit.[39] On several occasions, I have had the privilege of being a guest speaker for a meeting of a local chapter of Courage, combined with members of Encourage, persons who have family members struggling with same-sex attractions and who support members of Courage. The testimonies following my presentation struck me by the prevalence of "father issues" which were shared. My own clinical work with many individuals who are likewise struggling with same-sex attractions further corroborates the importance of this issue.

And the debate goes on. In May 2001, the Associated Press reported research led by Dr. Robert L. Spitzer, professor of psychiatry at Columbia University, which he presented in New Orleans before the meeting of the American Psychiatric Association. Dr. Spitzer, who apparently led the charge in 1973 when the American Psychiatric Association decided to remove homosexuality from the list of mental disorders, called at that time for studies on whether some people can change their sexual orientation. Spitzer, who does not himself offer reparative therapy, comments that when he began his research, he was skeptical about the possibility of changing sexual orientation. He interviewed by telephone 200 persons averaging 43 years of age, including 143 men and 57 women, who claimed that their sexual orientation had changed through reparative therapy. In the case of the men, this therapy took place over about 14 years, and 12 years in the case of the women. 66 percent of the men and 44 percent of the women he interviewed had arrived at good heterosexual functioning, which is defined by Dr. Spitzer as being in a sustained, loving heterosexual relationship within the past year and never or rarely thinking of somebody of the same sex during heterosexual intercourse. In addition, 89 percent of the men and 95 percent of the women interviewed claimed to be bothered only slightly or not at all by unwanted homosexual feelings. Only 11 percent of the men and 37 percent of the women reported the complete absence of homosexual attractions and other same-sex preference indicators. Multiple strategies had been used in this reparative therapy, primarily including sessions with a mental health professional and support groups. Many critical voices have already reacted to the study, from other mental health professionals to gay rights activists, who generally point out that the 200 "ex-gays" who participated in this study were referred by religious groups that condemn homosexuality and that they were treated by therapists "with a strong anti-gay bias." A strong motivation to change is clearly a significant factor, and Dr. Spitzer concludes that, while we cannot estimate what percentage of highly motivated gay people can change their sexual orientation, research "shows some people can change from gay to straight, and we ought to acknowledge that."[40]

What, then, can we conclude about the possibility or even the necessity of someone being able to change? About the "possibility," I heartily concur with the conclusions of Father John Harvey:

> From the combined testimony of secular professionals and religious counselors, one may draw the modest conclusion that some persons with a homosexual orientation can acquire a heterosexual one through a process of prayer, group support, and sound

therapy. This is not to say that everyone who seeks such change is able to attain it. It does not mean, moreover, that individuals who have traveled over into heterosexuality and, in many cases, have married will be immune from homosexual attractions.[41]

With regard to the "necessity" to "change," I again quote Father Harvey at some length:

> If homosexual orientation is an "objective disorder," as the Sacred Congregation for the Doctrine of the faith holds in its "Letter to the Bishops of the Catholic Church on the Pastoral Care of Homosexual Persons," then are not homosexual Catholics obliged to seek to change their sexual orientation? I respond that an obligation does not bind in conscience unless the moral law *clearly* demands it and the person is able to carry it out. Thus, the person with homosexual tendencies is bound to sexual abstinence by the gospel precept of chastity and to the means of practicing chastity, but he does not have an obligation to take steps to change his orientation. However desirable this change may be, we can give no guarantee in our present state of knowledge that if one were to follow a certain program and plan of life to change orientation it would always happen; since therefore, it cannot be proven that such change will inevitably occur if we do certain things, one cannot impose an obligation to take certain steps for such a change. The basic ethical principle applicable to this situation is that one cannot impose an obligation unless one is *certain* it exists.[42]

SCREENING AND FORMATION FOR THE PRIESTHOOD

Should someone who struggles with same-sex attractions be prevented from studying for the priesthood? If not, how far should he be expected to go to change his homosexual ways of thinking and feeling? So great is Dr. Gerard van den Aardweg's concern about the deeper implications of homosexual deficits that he concludes that, "as a rule, a homosexual orientation, whether acted out or experienced only in the private emotional life, must certainly be regarded as a contraindication to the supernatural source of priestly interests."[43] Noting that Courage does not make a change of orientation an obligatory goal, though it does stress the need to move away from homosexual ways of feeling and thinking, Father John Harvey states: "Persons aspiring to study for the priesthood or religious life should take the means mentioned above to repudiate the homosexual lifestyle and should study the official teaching of the Church on the issue of homosexual behavior." However, with regard to a candidate for the seminary with "a habit of masturbation involving homosexual fantasy," Father Harvey continues: "From my pastoral experience I believe that such a young man has deep-seated problems and that he should not enter the seminary until he has attended to the emotional problems that give rise to masturbation. Needless to add, he should also achieve control over the habit of masturbation."[44]

Certainly, there is much truth to strong assertions about the need for careful screening of those being admitted as candidates for the priesthood, continuing up to the point of their ordination. Father Paul Schaugnessy makes the comparison: "If a groom expressed hesitations to his bride as to 'sexuality and fidelity and what that means,' she would have excellent reason to doubt his sanity or good will or both—clearly a happy marriage is not in the cards."[45] Dr. Maria Valdes advocates a screening process before admission, with reappraisals at intervals during formation, up to one year before ordination. She also proposes a method of intensive treatment to identify and heal past and present emotions.[46] It is true to say that such thoroughness remains an ideal rather than a reality in pre-ordination formation programs.[47]

Perhaps the most balanced judgment on the admission to seminary of men of homosexual orientation comes from Dr. George Weigel. In his characteristically brilliant book, *The Courage to Be Catholic: Crisis, Reform, and the Future of the Church*, he writes:

> Much confused air would be cleared if the Church would declare that a man of homosexual orientation who is qualified intellectually, who has not made his homoerotic desires the center of his personality and identity, who has been living a chaste life for a sustained period of time, who recognizes that his homosexual desires are disordered and has shown evidence of mastering

them through spiritual disciplines, and who clearly manifests an understanding of the priest as a spiritual father is welcome as a candidate for the priesthood.[48]

If there is a growing number of seminarians who experience a predominantly same-sex attraction, what is the effect upon seminaries? Father Andrew Greeley, suspects, and I would agree, that the laity "would say it is one thing to accept a homosexual priest and quite another to accept a substantially homosexual clergy, many of whom are blatantly part of a gay subculture."[49] Father Cozzens gives his take on how this can be experienced in seminaries:

> Straight men in a predominantly or significantly gay environment commonly experience chronic destabilization, a common symptom of which is self doubt. . . . Unaware that his psyche senses a challenge to his own integration and identity—and therefore is standing on alert—he notices only a vague feeling of discomfort and a loss of psychic energy. The feeling that something is wrong may be pervasive and unrelenting. Even with healthy, close relationships with women and other straight men, the feeling that he is somehow out of sync, that he just doesn't seem to fit in with the others, may suggest to the seminarian that he is not called to the priesthood. . . . Seminary formation faculties, unsure how to address the disproportionate number of gays and the formational implications of the situation, generally choose to approach the topic indirectly and, more often than not, on an individual basis through spiritual direction or counseling. . . . Compounding the challenge, of course, are seminary faculties which include a disproportionate number of homosexually oriented persons.[50]

Father Cozzens seems to feel that, in a less than discrete way, many priests and seminarians have already "come out." While Father Cozzens cites the research of others (dated and skewed though it be), he strangely does not refer to his *own* experience as a seminary rector—a silence I find deafening.

Bishop Earl Boyea, former rector of the Pontifical College Josephinum in Columbus, Ohio, has also weighed in in response to Father Cozzens' book. Bishop Boyea states:

I believe an argument can be made that, by the usual psychological criteria, today's seminarians are healthier than their predecessors. Psychological counseling and spiritual formation programs are much more probing and exacting than was the case in former times. . . . As for Fr. Cozzens' depiction of seminarians, I can only say that they must be very different from those I have known during fourteen years of seminary work. Are there seminarians who identify themselves as homosexual? Certainly. Are there some who are sexually confused and in need of counseling and spiritual direction? Absolutely. But is there a dominant homosexual culture in seminaries that makes life difficult, if not impossible, for heterosexuals? That does not jibe with my experience. It is very possible that in the 1970s and '80s there were a significant number of seminarians who were sexually confused, and were encouraged in that confusion by a sexually charged society. They were not challenged to harmonize their ideas and lives with the teaching of the Church, and today some of them are priests. Some are effective and faithfully celibate, while some are actively involved in the gay subculture. The latter pose a very real problem, but the incidence of the problem, I am convinced, is nowhere near the figure proffered by Fr. Cozzens. His claims are both unsupported and irresponsible.[51]

To these various reports of others involved in priestly formation I wish to add my own twelve-year experience as a seminary rector, relying also on my psychoanalytic training. Over the years, I have made what I consider to be very serious efforts on my part to get to know each seminarian in formation, in order to get as deep an insight as possible into where he is with these issues before considering his preordination formation to be approaching completeness.[52] I do *not* think that a preponderate number of those in the seminary over the last ten years experience a predominantly same-sex attraction. I find them generally to be rather well rounded and as healthy as their peers outside the seminary, though, like their contemporaries, they often suffer some of the consequences of the devastation of family life in our society. I feel that my own impressions are corroborated by the psychological screening (including projective testing) required before admission, as well as by the experience I have of them in the classroom, in community life, and above all, in the chapel. I have not found any need of "tolerating the lavender" with them, as Father Andrew Greeley cutely insinuates,[53] though sometimes it has been hard to tolerate some of the sloppiness that can go along with a group of men living together. Generally, I find them displaying manly qualities; these days, more seem to be interested in sports and playing athletics, if that indicates anything. I lived in seminaries in the early seventies where campy humor saturated all the conversation, and the fresh air I breathe now in the absence of this is indeed refreshing. I occasionally still see a few who gather into cliques and begin to cultivate stinging and mutually debasing humor with sexual innuendo, but this is now so rare in the seminary that it sticks out like a sore thumb. I wish I could say it has become just as rare at some clergy gatherings. Several of the healthiest signs I can see among seminarians in their community life is that they do not tolerate that kind of talk and humor from each other, and it is among themselves rather than by a decree from on high that it is ordinarily weeded out. Now *that* is healthy!

Speaking of a sense of humor, one of the major delights I take in seminary community life these days is the usually good-natured and affectionate banter that is part of the steady diet of daily life. I have seen very shy individuals drawn out into the mainstream by the kind and caring ways their peers interact with them and engage them in conversation and activity. But it is not all light; there are frequent occasions for deeper discussions about things that have taken place in pastoral situations or are treated in the classroom. They also share with each other their own journeys, past and present, as well as requests to pray for family members or other acquaintances in need. They certainly struggle with issues, including celibacy, but seem comfortable discussing this with each other as well as with their spiritual director. More often than not, their struggle has to do with a desire to marry and have children. Surely, there are men among them who have experienced some of the deficits in their relationships with men, and perhaps with women, that we have analyzed in trying to understand same-sex orientation. But is not this healthy, male environment, where there is openness and the availability of genuine affection and care, an excellent healing atmosphere for such individuals and surely for us all in our growth to wholeness?

This healing environment is supplemented, of course, by inter-relationships with women: those women who serve not only as secretaries but as professors of subjects, including such personal issues as spirituality; those who exercise authority over them, such as academic deans and field education supervisors; and those with whom the seminarians experience and engage in theological reflection in some classes and pastoral ministry. Such is my overwhelming experience, and while it surely is far from perfect, this is its basic tenor.

Nonetheless, it has become painfully clear during our times that the ordained priesthood has become afflicted at its very heart through sexual misconduct. The solution does not lie in changing our understanding of priesthood or the way it is lived, nor is elimination of the discipline of celibacy going to relieve this deep affliction. Rather, there must be a recovery of the meaning of priestly celibacy and a renewal of priestly life by a radical deepening of the self-emptying love that configures the priest to Christ in his very heart.

CHAPTER FIVE

The UNCHANGING PRIESTLY HEART

Celibacy and Intimacy

CELIBACY AND THE PRIESTHOOD
The Evangelical Counsels

We have already had many occasions to discuss priestly celibacy as we have considered issues pertaining to power and sexuality. We have mentioned that celibacy is perhaps the aspect of priestly life most often brought up when discussing whether the Catholic priesthood is in crisis. We now want to consider the challenge and the gift which celibacy is: first, as it is presented in the life of Jesus, and then, its place in the call He issued, "Follow me."

Priestly Ideals in the Old Law

The prophet Malachi, one of the last Old Testament prophets, presents the ideal for priests of the Old Law: that they take to heart the covenant of life and peace the Lord made with Levi and that, like Levi, they should emulate the fear of the Lord and awe of His name. The priest must have true doctrine in his mouth and no dishonesty on his lips, walking with the Lord in integrity and uprightness, turning many away from evil (cf. Mal. 2:1–6). Priests are bearers of knowledge and messengers of the Lord of hosts (cf. Mal. 2:6–7), offering instruction and judgment. To do so, they must have a profound sense of awe at God's transcendence

and humble fear before His law—all of this within a life of intimate and constant union with God, walking with Him in
integrity and righteousness.[1]

Most striking is the profound intimacy with the Lord and the
unique holiness that is called for in the very heart of the priest, particularly in the Deuteronomic tradition. Even in the priestly tradi-
tions, this holiness is not primarily thought of as being concerned
with what are known as "sexual taboos." Rather, it is in response to
the closeness of God, a total consecration to God and to the services that it is the duty and desire of the priest to offer Him.

> The divine transcendence and majesty are such as may be
> metaphorically called a devouring fire which claims entire posses-
> sion of those who devote themselves to it. . . . This total consecra-
> tion to Yahweh admitted for the Israelite priesthood that it should
> be wholly at the disposal of the Lord, implying the renunciation of
> temporal goods and the exercise of temporal, political activity. . . .
> Mission of reconciliation, mission of blessing, mission of instruc-
> tion, mission to set up on earth in a certain manner the court of
> Yahweh, and thus to place it, on the earthly level, next to the
> heavenly court, the angelic court, in a halo of holiness which was
> not only ritual but ethical; such are the features of Old Testament
> priesthood which the New Testament would endorse.[2]

New Testament

If "sexual taboos" are not a dominant feature of the Levitical
priesthood, how did celibacy come to be such a prominent feature
of the priesthood of Jesus Christ? In the call of Christ, celibacy for
the sake of the Gospel and the kingdom is not a taboo or a prohibition, but a call to freedom. Saint Paul said he wished to be free
from any attachments to people so as to be able to become a slave
for all of them (1 Cor. 9:19). How did Jesus issue this call, and
how is it freeing?

When the disciples had heard the ideal expressed by Jesus in
His teaching on divorce, they observed, "If such is the case of a
man with his wife, it is not expedient to marry." Jesus replied,

"Not all men can receive this precept, but only those to whom it is given. For there are eunuchs who have been so from birth, and there are eunuchs who have been made eunuchs by men, and there are eunuchs who have made themselves eunuchs for the sake of the kingdom of heaven. He who is able to receive this, let him receive it" (Mt. 19:10–12). Thus, continence for the sake of the kingdom of heaven is not set in opposition to marriage, nor is it based on a negative judgment in regard to the importance of marriage.[3] Indeed, celibacy for the sake of the kingdom is not fundamentally a requirement but a counsel, a gift with its own value, leading to a certain type of consecration of one's life so that one can live as Saint Paul did, pouring himself out like a libation (Phil. 2:17). Celibacy is free. When celibacy is taken solely as a requirement for priestly ordination, the heart of its meaning— that it is a free act of love—can be lost.

Likewise, an emphasis on what is being given up can cause the deepest meaning of celibacy to be lost; it can seem to be an "aloofness," set apart from love. In fact, priestly consecration is not being set aside *from* love but is being set aside *for* love, like the jealous love of the Lord for His people (2 Cor. 11:1) who are set apart for His love. Celibacy lived authentically is a witness to the way God loves us—the love of one who is set aside, yet who thereby is in a position to be "everything to every one" (1 Cor. 15:28).

In the New Testament, celibacy is also an eschatological sign, a sign that the former world is passing away (1 Cor. 7:29). Under the Old Covenant, sexuality was important not only for the continuation of the people but also to accomplish the birth of the hoped-for Messiah. "But an entirely new situation is created with the birth of Christ from the Virgin Mary, with his own virginal life, with his death, descent into hell and Resurrection from the dead. Sexuality has now attained its inner end, the further propagation of the species has now attained a kind of theological insignificance,"[4] a "disinterestedness in view of the kingdom of heaven."[5] Now the significance is to be found in a kind of "eschatological virginity," which is in anticipation of what is to come, when men and women will neither marry and be given in marriage (Mk. 12:25). Presently, we are called to be free from the anxieties and cares that come from the things of the world (Mt. 6:25), so that we can be "anxious about the affairs of the Lord" and please Him by our dedication (1 Cor. 7:32–33). Living out the nuptial meaning of the body in loving continence is a response to the call already within the human heart in the present temporal life, which causes us to yearn and to strive for our share in the future resurrection, when we shall see Him face-to-face. This loving continence witnesses to the fact that the body's end is not the grave but glorification.[6]

Is this face-to-face encounter with God a return to the original solitude in which man was created, from which God took him by creating a helper fit for him (Gen. 2:18)? Yet did man ever leave this original solitude before God, which he longs for as his glorification in the glory of God?

Continence for the sake of the kingdom reveals a unique fruitfulness, in imitation of the virginity of Christ's sonship and Mary's maternity. This fruitfulness is "different from that of the flesh, a fruitfulness of the Spirit: 'That which is conceived in her is of the Holy Spirit'" (Mt. 1:20).[7] This fruitfulness comes through restraining the consummation of a certain type of intersubjective communion, made possible by our dual nature in being created male and female. By our bodiliness, this restraint in fact bears the fruit of an even fuller form of intersubjective communion with others on earth and face-to-face with God in the kingdom—a fruitfulness mirroring the perfect intersubjective communion of the triune love of God.[8]

If the nuptial meaning of the body is our created, human possibility of being self-gift, then we can see how continence as self-gift for the sake of the kingdom is complementary to, and not in contradiction with, the procreative mutual self-gift of a man and a woman. Both celibate and married love are conjugal in the total self-gift that they entail—a loving, self-giving taking up of one's cross everyday in following Christ (Lk. 9:23). In this sense also, spiritual spousal love and spiritual paternity and maternity, in which one renounces marriage and a family of one's own,[9] are as real as the physical paternity, maternity, and spousal love that takes place in marriage and family life.

Man is distinct from all the animals, as his very awareness of his difference from all other living beings demonstrates. As we have seen, this places him beyond mere sexual instinct into the realm of a nuptial meaning, whereby he is conscious of his capacity to give himself freely through self-renunciation and thereby rediscover himself in the free gift of himself. The nuptial gift of self in continent love for the sake of the kingdom is really a gift of oneself to Christ, a continence in which the giver does not cease to be human but gives oneself with all the masculinity and femininity proper to one's sexual and personal subjectivity.[10] Cardinal Hans Urs von Balthasar affirms the appropriateness of the discipline of priestly celibacy, observing, "No one maintains that it could not be otherwise. But we would have to say that it is best the way it is."[11] Pope John Paul II even went beyond this in his theology of the body, pointing out not only that celibacy must be voluntary and that it is best the way it is, but also is in accord with the nuptial meaning of our humanity, as created in the image and likeness of God, and with our human capacity to make a gift of self. For Saint Paul, "pleas[ing] the Lord" (1 Cor. 7:32) has to do with loving Him. A man who is married also seeks to "please God," but as a husband, he must be anxious to please his wife as well; in this sense, he is divided by reason of his family obligations (cf. 1 Cor. 7:32–34). An unmarried man is free to strive for an "interior integration," a "unification" that allows a dedication to pleasing God in a more exclusive and total way, in all the dimensions of one's life.[12]

It goes without saying (but needs to be said) that one who is unmarried and undivided for the sake of the kingdom, out of an exclusive love of God, can become divided and even more distracted from love of God than someone who is married. Indeed, all love should take us outside ourselves and open us to what is beyond us; yet if one becomes closed in on oneself and seeks only to please oneself, then love dies and loveless emptiness results. If one's love is for God, one will love others in that love. The tragedy is to become divided in love, as can happen when married persons become divided in their love for each other by another person or by the pursuit of material or other objects of desire. So, too, dedicating oneself in an undivided way to please God can become divided by other loves, including love of self, thereby losing union with God. Indeed, these are the "temptations" on the way to the kingdom of which Jesus speaks (Lk. 22:28–29). Yet remaining united with the Lord and rejoicing in His presence is surely the goal of virginal continence and all manners of consecration, of setting oneself apart exclusively for God as a pure and spotless offering (cf. Eph. 5:27).[13] This is the holiness toward which priestly consecration is directed.

Apostolic Origins of Priestly Celibacy

Let us now look back to the concrete history by which this divine plan for us has been realized. There has been considerable debate regarding the practice of celibacy in the life of the Church. It has usually been held that married men were ordained priests as a matter of common practice in the East, as well as throughout much of the history of the Church in the West. This assertion is true. Yet to understand it, we need to distinguish between two words that we have been using: continence and celibacy. *Celibacy*, from the Latin *caelebs*, means "unmarried."[14] *Continence*, in this sense, means "sexually contained or abstinent." It is correct to assert that in the West the prohibition against ordaining married men came relatively late in the history of the Church, at the time of the reform of Pope Gregory VII and the Lateran Councils.[15] Celibacy in this sense was a twelfth-century innovation in the West. But throughout the earlier centuries, while married men could be ordained, all men ordained to higher orders were obligated to sexual continence, whether they were virginal, widowers, or married. For the first seven centuries of the history of the universal Church, both East and West observed this discipline of sexual continence for ordained men. It was a seventh-century innovation in the East for sexual continence only to be required of bishops as legislated by the Second Council of Trullo in the year 691.[16]

This call to embrace sexual continence in following Jesus more closely springs from the evangelical counsel of Jesus (Mt. 19:9–12), and the practical application of this by Saint Paul (1 Cor. 7) and the pastoral letters (1 Tim. 3; Tit. 1). Eventual legislation of this practice insists that this tradition goes back to apostolic times. In the West, this earliest legislation is found at the Spanish Council of Elvira in the year 306,[17] the Roman Synod in the year 385 (led by Pope Siricius), and the Council of Carthage in the years 390 and 401.[18] Legislation in the East, likewise claiming only to codify a discipline of sexual continence for deacons, priests, and bishops going back to apostolic times, is found in the Code of Justinian, including laws passed between the years 529 and 565, modified in the seventh century to only include bishops.[19] The conviction that this tradition of continence went back to the practice of the apostles themselves, whether they were married or unmarried, was also a conviction held by all leading theologians of the third and fourth centuries in both the East and the West,[20] including Pope St. Clement of Rome, Tertullian of Carthage, Saint Clement of Alexandria, Origen of Alexandria, Saint Eusebius of Caesarea, Epiphanius of Salamis, Saint Jerome, Saint John Chrysostom, Theodore of Mopsuestia, and others.[21]

When the practice of sexual continence for ordained clergy began to crystallize into legislation in the fourth century, it was not due to a pressure to relax the requirement of continence, but was directed against schismatic Donatists, Novationists, and Priscillians. These groups, known as rigorists, were yielding to a Manichaean tendency to disparage the body and sexuality in reaction to a laxity of clerical discipline with regard to continence after ordination![22] Indeed, there is no historical evidence of opposition to the discipline of clerical continence until the reaction of Priscillianist reformers in Spain in the late fourth century, which did call for a relaxation of the discipline, and the Novationist legend about why the first ecumenical council, the Council of Nicea, did not legislate on clerical continence.[23] In subsequent centuries, the Church again forged a middle path between rigorism and laxism.

It was only during the centuries leading up to and through the Reformation that an attack unlike any until that time took place upon the very legitimacy of the discipline of celibacy. It became one of the leading points of contention raised by the reformers, especially Zwingli and Luther.[24] There was now an increased need for the Church to present the deepest reasons for this practice even more effectively—often as a defense not only against the arguments of reformers but even against those within the Church, such as Desiderius Erasmus. This challenge was made even greater by the spiritual and intellectual climate of the time, which tended to assume a merely humanistic or naturalistic approach to understanding celibacy. This is not unlike many arguments in our own times against maintaining the discipline of celibacy, which are prone to ignore the reality of the supernatural life of grace and the importance of asceticism, instead wanting to make concessions to demands for an easier path.

Ultimately, the Church once again responded to the reformers by entering into a period of renewal, which flowered in the sixteenth century with the Council of Trent. Not only did this council renew the practice of celibacy, but it also undertook many measures to reform priestly life and to restore its relationship with the episcopacy.[25] This was furthered by an overall spiritual renewal of priestly life that came through the establishment of seminaries and oratories and the inspiration of persons like Jean Jacques Olier and Saint Vincent de Paul. The fruits of this Catholic Reformation would continue to nourish priestly life through the centuries of enlightenment and rationalism and up into the twentieth century.

During the second half of the past century, the discipline of celibacy once again came very much into question, especially in the decades immediately following Vatican Council II—a time of sexual revolution, intense secularization, and increased emphasis on personal expression and fulfillment.

Contemporary Challenges

In discussing issues surrounding sexuality and power, we have already had occasion to hear the opinions of various authors: some call for changes in the way priestly life is lived, and some even insist that these changes are necessary if the priesthood is to survive. Often chief among their concerns seems to be the discipline of celibacy: Are the sacrifices called for by celibacy too heavy for our times? Is there a need for a change in this requirement to create a healthier climate for seminary formation and priestly life?

In the spring semester of the academic year 2001, I taught for a course entitled "Celibacy, Sexuality, and Intimacy" for the first time. All of the students in the course were men studying for the priesthood. Much of the content of what I presented to them and of the animated discussions that took place in class is contained in this book. In the following pages, I will draw periodically upon some of their responses to the challenges seminarians recognize and face in living celibacy, as well as upon some of the other authors whom we have previously mentioned.

We have already made some observations on the many extraordinarily fine candidates presently preparing for the priesthood, particularly noting their readiness to sacrifice. Father Marzheuser of Saint Mary Seminary in Cincinnatti describes them as "world weary," many taking up priesthood as a second career because professional life did not satisfy them. Because the secular world seems to them lacking in values, these candidates enter formation for the priesthood wanting to make some serious sacrifices: "They cannot be recruited by appealing to a certain standard of living. Comforts and perks do not attract them; challenge does. . . . They may enter with an idealized notion of priesthood, but it is very unlike what previous generations would call 'putting priesthood on a pedestal.'"[26]

With regard to the sacrifices required to live celibately, it is important to know that these days few candidates for priesthood come because they were not able to enter into intimate relationships or to find someone whom they would like to marry. In my experience, they often have left a relationship with a woman whom they seriously considered marrying—a relationship that during difficult moments might even seriously compete with their attempts to make the sacrifice of living a celibate life, which they are already embracing in the seminary. Many tend to share the conviction expressed by one of my seminary students:

> I do not believe that the removal of celibacy would benefit the Church during the current shortage of vocations to the priesthood. Firstly, this shortage is not due to a lack of men being called to the priesthood, but rather from the lack of response to the calls that are being made by God. An answer to the call in our day represents such a tremendously radical response by the individual, and it truly is an amazing witness to Christ in our culture. Whereas parents once prayed for vocations for their children, today many parents are quite dismayed when their child responds to the call. Secondly, for the Church to renounce the discipline of celibacy (and his gift of celibacy from Christ to his Church) simply because of a current "numbers" problem would demonstrate a lack of faith that Christ will provide shepherds for his flock.

Indeed, a concern of mine has to do with a zeal that seems to keep seminarians as well as those who have been ordained for many years in constant overdrive. This can be aggravated by idealistically dichotomizing the supernatural and the natural, relying on grace in a way that can try to skate past the "hard work of human development" and the necessary process of caring for one's own psychological and physical well-being. As Father Marzheuser comments, "Some of them do not regard their own body as integral to their own identity. These often push their bodies to go on as little sleep as possible, believing that rest and holiness are inversely proportional. . . . These same men are surprised when they develop physical problems usually identified with stress."[27]

Many times present-day candidates for the priesthood do not find a fervent spirit of self-sacrifice in the clerical world around them. They can become confused when confronted with the sometimes flagrant "selfism" and galloping self-indulgence they had hoped to leave behind. Though they themselves find celibacy to be a formidable challenge, they are disappointed at the cries that the sacrifices of the priesthood are too great and that the discipline of celibacy must change. Mostly, they would say that the change that is needed lies not in abolishing or relaxing the discipline, but in reforming and renewing it. I do not find them unrealistic about how heavy the burdens and how daunting the challenges can be. It is their solution that makes the difference: faith and prayer.

For these seminarians, these are not pat answers, but a way of life they are already living, a way of life that has led them to recognize that living celibately is a gift, and one that can only be opened by grace. A significant watershed mentioned by many students in the transition to celibate life takes place in the movement from "simply holding on for dear life" to "enjoying the nature of the gift of celibacy."

Indeed, the practice of the discipline of priestly celibacy and the integration of celibate sexuality is a process of interior integration, as Pope John Paul II has described. At the same time, it is like the new wine that cannot be put into old wineskins. As with living the priestly vocation itself, living celibately requires profound and ongoing conversion. Celibacy must be worn as a seamless garment. No matter how holy he already may be, each individual priest is called to reform in every area of his priestly life, including his celibacy and sexuality, through courageous fraternal witness and support, so that more and more the priest will live as total self-gift. In the next chapter we will discuss further the process of ongoing reformation in priestly life.

INTIMACY AND THE PRIESTHOOD
Intimacy

The New Dictionary of Catholic Spirituality defines intimacy as "the experience of closeness or union between two persons."[28] The word *intimacy* comes from the Latin word *intimus*, meaning "innermost, most secret, close, most profound; intrinsic, essential; belonging to or characterizing one's deepest nature; marked by very close association, contact, or familiarity; marked by a warm friendship developing through long association; suggesting informal warmth or privacy; of a very personal or private nature."[29] One of my seminary students defines the conditions of intimacy in this way: "Communion, in exposure of persons to another, necessitates faith. Entrance into the innermost, most profound part of a person does not entail a conquering, but responds with motivating wonder and awe. Maybe herein lies a healthy fear granting the just respect of self and others."

We have already discussed the communion of love possible between two persons in mutual self-gift, flowing from the nuptial bodiliness of our humanity. How does this allow us to understand human intimacy? We might begin by saying that intimacy always involves some kind of mutuality. Indeed, the mutuality experienced in intimacy is such that it is as if, for that moment, the other was the only other person in the world. For intimacy to take place, the experience of mutuality must have established or been established upon trust. The quality of the "original" which we have seen in Pope John Paul's theology of the body is pervasive here; there is a nakedness and innocence in intimacy that has an originality to it. Intimacy is the experience of the capacity for and, to whatever degree, the realization of nuptiality in a mutual self-giving. As such, intimacy must always be reciprocally free.

Intimacy always involves sexuality because a person always must enter into mutuality through his or her bodiliness. All intimacy is sexual because all intimacy is bodily, whether or not genitality and sexual attraction are prominent. The sexual dimensions involved can be a profound impetus toward deepening intimacy; however, they can be the way in which intimacy is derailed into lust or some type of objectification of the other person. Sexual intimacy brings out the deeply personal vulnerability and nakedness of a reciprocal self-gift of persons, whether this is genitally consummated or not. One of my seminary students expressed this in a way that sweeps the spectrum from the ordinary to the extraordinary:

Some in contemporary society will scoff at the notion that one can express love for another via the body or make a gift of self without involving genital sexuality. It can be done and is done on a regular basis. Recalling that our primary means of communication with others is via the body and that, because of this, every relationship we have with other people is a sexual relationship, it follows that every time we help someone other than ourself, we are giving a gift of self. Visiting someone at the hospital, mourning someone at a funeral, offering someone advice on a critical life decision, or just playing a game of cards with someone are forms of self-gift. The unifying thread in these examples is the service we show others. People will come to us with problems and we are there for them to lend an ear to listen or to cry with them. No matter how uncomfortable it may make us feel, we are there to help the other person.

Intimacy is not easy to measure, though there are varying degrees in which it is realized. There is a certain intimacy just in being in the presence of another person, in a mutual awareness of each other's presence. Already, this presence to another involves vulnerability and implies receptivity. (Consider the alternative, when a person is not aware of or deliberately ignores the presence of another person.) The intimacy heightens through that most powerful sexual organ of the human body, the eyes, especially if the look is prolonged and extended by a willingness to disclose oneself and be discovered, allowing a rare vulnerability which may say much more than many words. Speaking can be intimate speech, especially if it is speech arising from reflective and responsive listening; it can even be more intimate when the speech arises from a listening silence within and between the two. One of my seminary students who had been practicing "active listening" in a class on pastoral counseling commented, "I found it simply amazing the torrents of conversation that would be released when people knew that you were actually, really listening to what they had to say." Intimacy involves a sharing and exposure of oneself to another, revealing one's deepest personal self.

A relationship forms when a continuity of intimate experiences, webbed together across the vulnerable spaces of separations
and absences, form invisible bonds of friendship, love, and trust,
which grow and bridge the chasms between the unseen and the
seen. Such bonds of friendship are deepened in times of solitude
alternating with experiences of intimacy. Although intimacy cannot fill the solitude, solitude cannot ever obliterate intimacy,
which spans the expanse of time and reaches out to eternity. There
is then a communion of persons, which is true intimacy. It is our
human nuptial capacity for self-gift which undertakes the risks
that make this intimacy possible. In the divine plan, human persons are capable of entering into the mutuality of intimacy in a
way that is somehow always a "coming home," even within the
irreplaceable uniqueness of each relationship and within the
unrepeatable newness of each further encounter. The mystery of
intimacy is the mystery of love, always opening up the spiritual
dimensions of each person and revealing the divine intimacy
reflected in any human relationship.

We have emphasized mutuality in intimacy; but can there be
intimacy without mutuality? Mutuality is never perfectly symmet-
rical, and the intimacy which two persons seek is often elusive and
fleeting. It would seem that great and mature love must venture
forth toward the other in a way that is self-disinterested, often
doing without the desired response or even without any response
or reciprocity at all. But is this intimacy, if there is no response
from the other? It seems to me that love can be intimate even
without the awareness and response of the other person to the love
and self-gift that is being extended. Indeed, this would seem to be
always possible in the vulnerability inherent in intimate love. As
Franciscan Friar of the Renewal Father Benedict Groeschel has
expressed it:

> If you want to love, you must be willing to be vulnerable. The
> Gospel makes it clear that if you extend your hand often enough
> in a gesture of love, someone will drive a nail through it. If you

love others, you may be deceived, betrayed and abandoned. If you love Christ, you must walk the difficult road to Calvary. But you will begin to see yourself borne by powers that are beyond you. It may not be very noticeable at first. It may be no more than patience with criticism, or extra generosity after you have done enough. You may feel firmly drawn to God even when you can't pray. You will begin to change. And this is the effect of charity, which will overflow into a love for others that goes beyond affection or pity.[30]

These experiences of intimacy between persons take us into the realm of celibate intimacy, which is godlike in that it loves first, often without the reciprocity for which love longs so deeply. The pain of love that goes unrecognized or even scorned, or which the other person is simply unable to reciprocate, can still have the intimacy of self-gift, even of total self-gift. As we have just said, this intimacy flows from a very godly way of loving.

Celibate Intimacy

The communion possible between two persons in mutual self-gift, flowing from the nuptial bodiliness of our humanity, can be dedicated in an undivided way to "pleasing" God, with an exclusivity not possible to those who are pleasing God by pleasing family and spouse. As one of my seminary students expressed it,

The thing I value most about celibacy is that I can be present to all people, young and old, male and female, and I can be involved with them in a way that is both "safe" for me (in the sense that I have a commitment to the Lord), and "safe" for them (they understand my commitment to the Lord), allowing for a giving of myself to all those present to me at a given time. I think that celibacy does affect intimacy in that it must allow for an expression of intimacy in a way that is oriented for all, available to all, and not locked into a single relationship or person. But this sort of intimacy allows for greater levels of relationship with a greater number of people.

Many seminarians recognize that priests "have the opportunity to have a dynamic of intimacy with people often deeper than the intimacy of a married couple engaged in sexual intercourse. People turn to their priests during the most emotional points in their lives: the birth of a newborn, marriage, and death are just a few examples." This certainly resonates with my own experience as a priest. I can no longer count the number of times in my priestly ministry when someone has said to me, "I have never been able to tell that to anyone before. You are the only person with whom I have ever been able to share that."

At the same time, seminarians are usually well aware of the challenges and the cost. As one seminarian relates: "Raised in the generational culture of the '80s and '90s, I believe the most difficult facet of celibate life I will have to face in the future is overcoming the inculcated opinion that to be normal is to have sex and to have it very often. However, it is this very opportunity which draws me to celibacy." Another comments:

The most difficult part of celibacy is the times of loneliness in which the longing for the comfort of a single other person, in intimate and even sexual ways, is present. There can be great sufferings when one sees nephews and nieces, or other young families and the natural longings for those very things are manifest in the heart. I think that there is a certain level of "being alone" that is inherent in the celibate vocation. The idea of growing older without another person, or even not having a particular focus for love can be difficult. There is also the fear that perhaps there will be failure in the celibate vocation, failing to live out the promises made before God and the family of God.

"Both in life and death, we are the Lord's"; yet the celibate belongs to the Lord in such a way that he belongs to no one else. Capuchin Father Keith Clark notes that committed celibate persons can have as many moments of intimacy in their lives as single or married persons do. He qualifies what he means by celibate intimacy by telling what a female friend said to him about himself and about another priest, Ralph, who was leaving to get married: "You don't belong to anybody, Keith Clark, and you never should! Ralph used to belong to all of us, but now he belongs to Jennifer."[31] As one of my seminary students observed, "The grace of celibacy allows a priest to give himself as if each person he encounters is the only person in the world." The intimacy of the celibate with God has an integration that is unified and undivided, freeing Him to love others in a way like that in which God loves us: as if each one were the only person in the world. Now that is intimacy! And He loves each one of us that way!

The practice of celibate intimacy unfolds in a life of faith and prayer. All persons can pray and must have faith in God, but the one exclusively devoted to pleasing God can enter into prayer in a way that can be more focused and less distracted by other relationships with the persons one loves. This is true regardless of whether or not I am personally successful in freeing myself of distractions during prayer on any particular day, since prayer is never a merely human activity. In prayer, as Pope John Paul II writes, "the true protagonist is God."[32] Thus, the intimacy in prayer flows within the mutuality of God's sharing Himself with me in a personal way. He is the One who initiates the relationship, and I am naked and vulnerable before Him. Celibate prayer takes place within an undivided intimacy of spousal love of the one consecrated or set apart exclusively for this relationship. As such, celibate prayer and intimacy should be able to be less distracted and more prolonged because it flows from a more exclusive version of the relationship which all persons have in some way with God, and which all Christians have through the person of Jesus Christ. This celibate intimacy bears the fruit that is so essential to priestly life and ministry—praise, adoration, and glory.

Purity of Heart and Autoeroticism

Saint Paul states it boldly: "[T]he immoral man sins against his own body" (1 Cor. 6:18); "The body is not meant for immorality, but for the Lord, and the Lord for the body" (1 Cor. 6:13). He then elaborates: "For, as it is written, 'The two shall become one [flesh].' But he who is united to the Lord becomes one spirit with him" (1 Cor. 6:16–17). Purity of heart cannot only be "sometimes," but requires disposition and constancy for the heart to become one. The disposition of this constancy is purity, purity of heart. There are two dimensions of purity, as Pope John Paul points out, "the moral dimension, or virtue, and the charismatic dimension, namely the gift of the Holy Spirit."[33] We have discussed many aspects of sexuality, eventually bringing them into our reflection on priestly life and celibacy. Our entire approach to sexuality and to love has, of course, focused on relationships between two persons. But what about autoeroticism, sexual pleasure that actually takes place alone, involving only my own body and myself?

Research has indicated that "among Americans aged eighteen to fifty-nine, about 60 percent of the men and 40 percent of the women had masturbated during the past year. About one man in four and one woman in ten reported that they masturbate at least once a week. And these are not adolescents, they are adults, most of whom have regular partners for sexual intercourse."[34] Therefore, while many believe that "most scientific opinion holds that it [masturbation] can be a normal and healthy sexual outlet throughout life unless complicated with some admixture of excessive guilt, compulsion, social isolation, or misaligned fantasy life,"[35] the facts would seem to contradict the hypothesis that people masturbate to relieve the sexual tension they are not expressing, since those "whom the substitute-outlet theory says are most likely to masturbate actually masturbate the least and those who are supposed to masturbate the least do it the most. In that sense, masturbation is like using erotica and having frequent thoughts of sex—not as an outlet so much as a component of a sexually active lifestyle."[36]

We cannot dismiss problems over the meaning and morality of masturbation by blaming the negative Christian approach to it.[37] Nor can the matter be resolved by caricaturizing how it was seen as "the most unnatural behavior, . . . more unnatural than fornication or adultery . . . , 'the greatest sin'. . . of 'self-abuse' or 'pollution.'" Neither should it be dismissed by suggesting that now most "people and many priests . . . do not consider masturbation ordinarily sinful."[38] Despite a more libertine attitude, it does not seem that the absence or presence of "guilt" is the main thing going on in masturbation, since research shows that only "about half of the men and women who masturbated said they felt guilty. . . . Yet, for 'men' at least, the frequency of masturbation for those who felt guilt was very similar for those who did not."[39] Also, despite the assertions that masturbation correlates with introversion and social isolation, masturbation is in fact found especially among those who seek out more sexual experiences in general, and also those who experiment with a greater variety of sexual experiences.[40] Strangely, however, the research we have been citing, while recognizing that the frequency of masturbation is not strongly correlated to guilt, goes on to conclude that "the practice [of masturbation] is so strongly influenced by social attitudes that it becomes more a reflection of a person's religion and social class than a hidden outlet for sexual tensions,"[41] but does not go on to correlate it with the level of sexual activity and experimentation.

What about images and "erotica" that excite sexual feelings in the beholder? What is pornography, and when is the body being presented pornographically? In his theology of the body Pope John Paul II analyzes the crucial distinction between nudity as seen in a work of art and nudity as it is seen pornographically:

A question arises: when and in what case is this sphere of man's activity . . . regarded as pornovision, just as in literature some writings were and are often regarded as pornography. . . .

Both take place when the limit of shame is overstepped, . . . when in the work of art or by means of audiovisual reproduction the right to the privacy of the body in its masculinity or femininity is violated. . . .

In the course of the various eras, beginning from antiquity— and above all in the great period of Greek classical art—there are works of art whose subject is the human body in its nakedness.

The contemplation of this makes it possible to concentrate, in a way, on the whole truth of man, on the dignity and the beauty— also the "suprasensual" beauty—of his masculinity and femininity. These works bear within them, almost hidden, an element of sublimation. This leads the viewer, through the body, to the whole personal mystery of man. In contact with these works, where we do not feel drawn by their content to "looking lustfully," which the Sermon on the Mount speaks about, we learn in a way that nuptial meaning of the body which corresponds to, and is the measure of, "purity of heart."[42]

Sadly, many persons feel that entertaining or conjuring up sexual images or thoughts—the "impure thoughts" of yesteryear—is no longer sinful. It goes right along with this that many consider the practice of masturbation to be a normal and healthy outlet, and the use of pornography to be normal if only viewed occasionally. Even more sadly, some priests have felt entitled to counsel penitents that these things are not really sinful, encouraging a freer attitude toward getting in touch with one's feelings and sexuality in order to loosen up or relieve tension. Perhaps this comes from a more permissive attitude that priests assume toward themselves in these matters.

In fact, in order to live chastely, we must cultivate purity of heart. Even short of compulsive and repetitive masturbation or use of pornography (the latter of these now reaching epidemic proportions thanks to the Internet), it is simply a fact that occupying my mind or imagination in these ways, even though I may seem to be "just taking a break from reality" and withdrawing into myself, affects the rest of my life. Consider the strain placed upon my actual relationship with someone about whom I have been fantasizing sexually. In order to live celibately and chastely, I must strive to live purely from my heart, in a way that includes my own mind, imagination, and body. Otherwise, I have already sinned in my own heart, even if I do so alone. Such turning inward and making myself or my fantasy the object of sexual pleasure is a movement in precisely the opposite direction from that which is made possible by our human nuptiality: the capacity for self-gift, for intimacy with a real human other in the reality of my personal life, and in intimacy with God as the real, divine Person who grounds all reality. To spend time—sometimes a great deal of time—in the realm of the imaginary can turn me inward, make me selfish, and reinforce my tendencies to objectify, thus forming habits of escape from reality by which I take back the gift of myself. To do so is to refuse to give back what I have been given, is to refuse the intimacy without which no human life, and surely no priestly life, can be lived. It is to refuse to make a free and total gift of myself, a gift that can only be given in purity of heart.

Celibate Intimacy and the Spiritual Life

We conclude this chapter with a final reflection on the spiritual meaning of the body, sexuality, and celibate intimacy. We have already considered the response of Jesus to a trick question about the resurrection of the body, in which He reproves His interrogators:

> Is not this why you are wrong, that you know neither the scriptures nor the power of God? For when they rise from the dead, they neither marry nor are given in marriage, but are like the angels in heaven. And as for the dead being raised, have you not read in the book of Moses, in the passage about the bush, how God said to him, 'I am the God of Abraham, and the God of Isaac, and the God of Jacob?' He is not God of the dead, but of the living; you are quite wrong." (Mk. 12: 24–27)

This conversation of Jesus with the Sadducees, recounted by all three of the Synoptic Gospels, is considered by Pope John Paul II in discussing the spiritual combat in which we are engaged, especially involving our body and our sexuality, as well as our search for intimacy and the eschatological meaning of priestly life:

> The reciprocal gift of oneself to God—a gift in which man will concentrate and express all the energies of his own personal and at the same time psychosomatic subjectivity—will be in response

to God's gift of himself to man. In this mutual gift of himself by man, a gift which will become completely and definitively beatifying, as a response worthy of a personal subject to God's gift of Himself, virginity, or rather the virginal state of the body, will be totally manifested as the eschatological fulfillment of the nuptial meaning of the body, as the specific sign and the authentic expression of all personal subjectivity.[43]

CHAPTER SIX

The EVER-EXPANDING PRIESTLY HEART

Priestly and Spiritual Renewal

*A*t the Chrism Mass on Holy Thursday, April 12, 2001, Pope John Paul II called upon bishops and priests to be saints, for the testimony they can give to Christian communities in the world depends on their holiness. He noted that "the priesthood and episcopacy is a road to sanctity. It is a road that each one travels in a very personal way, known only to God, who searches and knows hearts. . . . Although it is true that no one can become a saint in someone else's place, it is also true that each one must become a saint with and for others, following Christ's model." He went on to ask, "Is not personal sanctity nourished by that spirituality of communion, which must always precede and accompany concrete initiatives of charity? To educate the faithful [in holiness], we pastors are asked to give consistent witness."[1]

The sad thing is that many priests and not a few bishops might say or feel that this ideal is too lofty, too out of reach. The even sadder thing is that too often the exterior works and preoccupations of life bury any interiority in the ministry of priests and bishops. Finally, as we have seen, there is the great danger that what is done, even if it is somehow grounded and rooted in an interior life, is not totally focused on Christ. Let us consider the dimensions of priestly spirituality, especially from the perspective of what we have already seen about the unchanging heart of the priesthood. We shall first look at formation for priestly spirituality by examining further the situation among seminarians and those recently ordained in our time. I focus upon these two groups not only because they are the hope of the future but because they are sometimes misunderstood and misrepresented. We then will move on to further reflections on some elements of priestly spirituality and the process of ongoing spiritual formation throughout the life of a priest.

THE FUTURE OF PRIESTLY SPIRITUALITY AND RENEWAL
Seminarians

In earlier chapters, we made some remarks about present-day seminarians in terms of their sexual integration: their disposition toward celibacy, homosexuality, and other issues. The greatest strength I see in those answering the Lord's call in these times is their hunger for things spiritual and the considerable experience in the spiritual life that they bring with them when they come to the seminary. I have been humbled daily at the transparency of the spiritual journeys and ongoing conversion of men in the seminary today. It is so easy to get to know and love them. When Scott Hahn first began to teach at Saint Vincent Seminary as professor of Biblical Theology and Liturgical Proclamation, I told him that the best part of doing seminary work these days is the seminarians themselves. On the night of his final lecture of that semester, Professor Hahn heartily agreed with me and told me how he was sorry to see the course end, considering how readily he had come to know and become engaged with his students.

Present-day seminarians are sometimes characterized as theologically narrow and "doctrinaire," which, if true, would certainly not bode well for their ongoing conversion and formation, nor for their integration into the presbyterate and larger Church. I find myself very much in agreement with Father Richard Marzheuser (who until his death was academic dean of Mount Saint Mary Seminary of the West in Cincinnati) in his assessment that this new generation of seminarians is on the rise:

[They] are not anti-intellectual (like some earlier classes of students). They study hard [Remember this assessment is coming from an academic dean!], they think, ask questions, and they are not afraid to haggle with faculty in class or in conversation; but they are suspicious of things contemporary as if they were the mere product of shallow trends that are just passing through. They prefer to know more about the "tried and true": Patristic and Thomistic theology, the wisdom of the saints and papal teaching. They cannot get enough of that. They were raised on contemporary attempts at theology and they found them wanting.[2]

And they do love to talk, especially about matters to which they are strongly committed. I remember a time in seminary when no one was quite sure what he was committed to and did not feel all that comfortable talking about it unless it questioned what was established. Yes, there is a lot of talking, but there is also a lot of listening, and when the conversation at table or in the lounge goes on for hours they are talking about a lot more than the Steelers, though football probably comes into the conversation. One of the most astounding and least often remarked upon aspects of today's seminarians and recently ordained priests is their readiness and eagerness to share their faith. As Father Marzheuser observes,

Getting to know them is rather easy because these recent students are quite candid about their vocational biography: the spiritual experiences of their call, their family background, education and job history. . . . Many of them speak quite frankly of *mystical experiences* associated with the call they are following. By "mystical experience" they generally mean a specific moment of intense feeling and thought in which they received a direct spiritual communication. . . . . This is significant because, as far as I am aware, my generation (who entered seminary formation after Vatican II) and the one ahead of us never spoke of mystical experiences leading us to the seminary. . . . As far as I know, no other generation of priests speaks in these terms. Most priests are down to earth, ordinary, and concrete, and they expect to experience grace in the same way, not in unusual experiences because that is not how their vocation happened. What is at stake here is the style of ministry. If mystical experiences are one's own norm, then it is tempting to lead others to expect the miraculous as well. Those who expect the miraculous do preaching, presiding, spiritual direction, leadership, devotions, counseling, etc., differently than those who expect grace to be ordinary.[3]

There are built-in tensions here, tensions between generations of priests and in the way conversion does or does not take place. Father Marzheuser notes other significant differences in present-day seminarians:

> Pope John Paul II also figures prominently in their vocational consciousness. . . . Many of them come to seminary out of the Right to Life movement. . . . Their activism and motivation carries over into other causes as well, such as cross-cultural awareness, protesting capital punishment, inclusion of the disabled, etc. . . . They have come to abhor passivity (a critique they make of the generations ahead of them), . . . they are activists. . . . Together, these make them very restless. The "activities" of the seminary do not measure up to the life and death issues that they are accustomed to addressing. If vocation is measured by *passion*, many of them feel they are ready for ordination now. Many of them are what I would call "*world weary.*" In their lives the world is not a place which supports faith. On the contrary, the world seems to be chipping away at the faith all the time, and this constant barrage wears them out. They blame the secularization of culture for this negative experience. . . . These men have a great love for the Church. It may be idealistic and in some cases, even naive, but what they hunger for most is civility and equilibrium.[4]

Whether they have mostly come from a deeply Catholic background, as Father Marzheuser experienced,[5] or whether most have undergone profound conversion later in life, as have more of the seminarians with whom I have dealt, there is no mystery about what got them there and what keeps them going: their spiritual life, usually unfolding in a deeply personal way in relationship to the Lord and, more often than not, within a profound intimacy with the Lord in the Eucharist. This not only includes love for the daily celebration of the Eucharist, which remains central for them in such a way that it is seldom necessary for those in charge of their formation to insist upon it, but also extends to Eucharistic-centered prayer and devotion. I have found that the desire of this generation of seminarians for a more contemplative and silent prayer, which at the same time is less abstract and intellectual, is what has drawn them to the more tangible aspects of Eucharistic exposition and adoration. It is really an attempt to bring together the tangible and the transcendent:

> The Eucharist becomes the focus of this hunger because it is the most other-worldly thing they do as Catholics. Thus, the reserved presence remains the primary door to all spiritual realities. . . . The devotion of exposition is the way of giving flesh to and safeguarding this faith in the Eucharist. . . . They are inclined much more toward Eucharist as mystical experience, than Eucharist as communal worship. . . . They love to pray. It is not likely that they will lose their sense of balance here very often. Prayer is built into their rhythm before they enter the seminary; it's not something we taught them. Many of them come to us already committed to the Liturgy of the Hours, for instance, and much more. They dedicate a significant amount of time to prayer each day. Some will push themselves to get by on as little sleep as possible so they can dedicate even more time to prayer. I suspect that this has something to do with emulating John Paul II.[6]

In many ways, it is not surprising when this emphasis upon sacramental and devotional prayer becomes one of the most striking differences between seminarians of these days and those of just ten or fifteen years ago. Father Marzheuser once again offers excellent insights into this:

> We Catholics are an inherently sacramental, incarnate people. . . . We need to see, hear, touch and taste who we are, so that we know and remember it, but also so that our identity becomes "real" in the world. This is precisely what ritual does. The desire for the

multiplication of rituals (rosary, novenas, Eucharistic adoration, way of the cross, plus Marian and other devotions in addition to daily Eucharist and Liturgy of the Hours) is an indication that something is missing for this generation.[7]

The need to make prayer and love explicit is a reflection of the concreteness of persons of this generation, which actually has profound affinity with the Incarnation. We should be slow to diagnose this as a penchant for the externals or as superstition. These phenomena may be going in precisely the opposite direction in terms of genuinely personal spiritual appropriation.

As we have already discussed with regard to sexual and personal integration, a deep relationship with the Lord, which such a spiritual life allows, is undoubtedly the single greatest source of healing in the life of someone growing in integrity in his personal and sexual life. The strength of the spiritual life among seminarians and the recently ordained is the greatest reason for optimism, and the only solution to whatever "crisis of soul" there may be or will ever be in the priesthood. I am in profound agreement with the impressions of Father Marzheuser and do not identify the present situation or the future of the priesthood as in crisis, but as in need of reform, a reform which should not so much change the priesthood as it should call for change within the life of the priest. Any seminarian who is not open and eager for such change is not a suitable candidate for the priesthood, and any priest whose spiritual life is not vital enough to sustain ongoing reformation of life is at serious vocational risk.

We have been discussing seminarians primarily, and I have been presenting a rather positive outlook. In one way, I wish I could say that this is because Saint Vincent Seminary is an extraordinarily better seminary. I do feel we have an exceptional faculty, formation program, and community of seminarians, but I am convinced from my visits to many other seminaries that Saint Vincent is not that unique. The men who are answering the call to priesthood just now are the ones who are unique.

The Newly Ordained Priests

It is my strong impression that the corps of recently ordained reflects the same encouraging picture and that there is much more room for hope than discouragement. There are nevertheless some serious problems among the newly ordained, just as there are among seminarians. If there are problems over homosexuality and celibacy, these are indeed problems that should have approached some resolution in the seminary and often did not. However, I am convinced that the single weakest link in the priestly formation chain is the transition from seminary to priestly life and ministry. The number of vocational fatalities during this transition is alarmingly high, and many are related to sexuality and celibacy, at least in part. The experience of community in seminary is generally deeply appreciated by seminarians these days; often they can come to profoundly miss the friendships and deep relationships of seminary days, finding them difficult to replicate or replace in the context of parish life. Priests need good friendship with other priests, and this need cannot fully be supplied by the more readily available relationships with other persons met within and outside of priestly ministry (PDV 120–21).

Many bishops and pastors, as well as the congregations of these recently ordained priests, understandably ask whether the seminary is at fault for failing to solve these problems in their pre-ordination formation. The seminary faculty ask themselves this question, yet wonder whether there is also failure on the part of the diocese to choose first assignments wisely—not so much to provide the perfect first experience of parish as to facilitate through mentoring and orientation an adequate transition to the complexities of ministry that can only be addressed once the man is actually ordained. Many issues, including sexual problems and questions over celibacy, can surface in a different and more poignant way than they did in the seminary, with its community life and regular schedule of prayer and spiritual direction. Are there support systems to orientate and help them start out in their diocesan ministry? Are there ways that the seminary and the diocese can continue to collaborate to help the newly ordained build a stronger community, one that prays and works together right from the start in their first assignment?

Adjusting to rectory life has very often turned out to be difficult for recently ordained priests. There are a variety of reasons for this. Many of these men lived alone before coming to the seminary, and no matter how much they responded to the opportunity to build fraternal bonds and enter into seminary community life, they can easily revert to living as if alone once they move into a rectory situation with one other man, particularly if he himself is a loner or if they don't get along. Another factor is the outspoken character of these men and the friction this can produce:

> Most of these men are transparent. They are not two-faced where they put up a facade while their real ecclesial self remains hidden or submerged. If they do not like something or disagree, they let you know it, and sometimes that is fairly often but I would much rather have the challenges that come with their transparency. . . . Some may not like what they see, but this generation does not play games with who they are. . . . They are motivated; they are energetic and full of ideas and I do not expect their zeal for the Faith or the Church to die out any time soon.[8]

There is also the question of clerical dress: there is clearly a greater likelihood for the newly ordained to "wear their collar" or even to wear a cassock. News from the front even reports that a few birettas have been sighted. What is this all about? Some who have been ordained for a few years look at all this with some concern and smell clericalism, perhaps mixed with nostalgia for a lost golden age these men never knew. Yet it seems to me that these are not usually the issues. I once again heartily agree with Father Marzheuser that these recently ordained "take for granted that faith is a sign of contradiction; that faith is counter-cultural. I believe that this is the proper context for their attraction to *clerical dress*. This is not the clericalism of former times where the collar represented a privileged identity—quite the opposite. The collar for this generation is a prophetic symbol thrust in the face of a secular world as a direct challenge to its values."[9]

Many newly ordained priests are confused by the lifestyle they find as they enter into priestly life. They recognize that there is a profound and dramatic need to restore simplicity to priestly life. As Father Schaugnessy points out, "Physical comfort is the oxygen which feeds the fire of . . . indulgence. Cut it off. When you enter a rectory, take a look at the liquor cabinet, the videos, the wardrobe, the slick magazines, and ask yourself, 'Do I get the impression that the man who lives here is in the habit of saying no to himself?' If the answer is negative, the chances are that the life of chastity is in disorder as well."[10] Perhaps these reflections sound like a monastic ideal is being superimposed upon the life of a diocesan priest. Indeed, this criticism is often levied by those who call for a radical renewal of priestly life, and especially of diocesan parish priestly life as we know it.

ELEMENTS OF PRIESTLY SPIRITUALITY
A Monastic Spirituality?

In *The Changing Face of the Priesthood*, Father Donald Cozzens once again drags out the old accusation that seminary formation has been inadequate because it was an imposition of a "monastic" spirituality not suited for diocesan priestly life and ministry. I suppose most of those who feel that way also feel that the pontificate of Pope John Paul II and recent magisterial teaching on priestly spirituality contributed to the problem by perpetuating the mistake. *Pastores Dabo Vobis* indeed reflects the very elements of priestly spirituality that are often rejected as "monastic"; moreover, I keep waiting for the critics to come forth with a more suitable spirituality, one which is truly, profoundly Catholic and priestly. I personally am convinced that diocesan priestly spirituality can find a complete presentation of the essential elements in *The Directory for the Life and Ministry of Priests*, issued in 1994 by the Vatican Congregation for Universities and Seminaries, and in, *Pastores Dabo Vobis*. One seldom hears these referred to enough, and not at all by Father Cozzens, at least in this particular work of his.

I am convinced that the problem is not that the wrong *kind* of spirituality has been imposed on diocesan priests from outside, but that there has been a wholesale abandonment of *any* spirituality that could ground radical conversion, which has led to a crisis within diocesan priestly life that has indeed reached disastrous proportions.[11] In terms of the effects of monastic spirituality upon priestly formation, Father Jean Galot observes that

> If monasticism prompted the priest to estrange himself externally from the world, if it drove him toward a spirituality marked by a low estimate of the world, then to this extent the impact of monasticism has been regrettable. But monasticism also contributed to a keener discernment of what is implied by the demands the gospel makes upon those who are called to follow Christ, just as the priestly ministry in turn helped religious to achieve a keener realization of their apostolic mission.[12]

Jesuit Father George A. Aschenbrenner, writing about diocesan priestly spirituality, even calls for a "monasticism of the heart," saying how this "radical monasticism of the heart—a stark aloneness with God in Jesus—must serve as bedrock for both the active and the monastic lifestyles. . . . The integration of the appropriate external, active spirituality with this profound monasticism of the heart makes possible a discerning sensitivity that can transform the busy priest's ministry from a shallow activism into a focused and unified life."[13]

Kenosis and the Evangelical Counsels

What is the spirituality of the priesthood that Father Cozzens proposes in place of the monastic spirituality and the spirituality before Vatican II, which he eschews? It is very evident that Father Cozzens does love and understand the priesthood in many ways. He respects the dedication, heroic struggles, and successes of priests in general and has sympathy for their weaknesses and failings. He also upholds the importance of a relationship with God in the life of the priest, insisting on the value and power of this. Yet here a certain shallowness pervades his writings, which perhaps does give a clue as to why he totally overlooks or misunderstands certain things.

Perhaps, as Father Benedict Groeschel suggests, the heart of the problem lies in Father Cozzens' notion of a relationship with God as "transcendence" in some abstract, philosophical sense. Father Cozzens describes transcendence as "those elusive moments in which we experience, literally, an unspeakable, harmonious, liberating union with creation. . . . One feels both infinitely small as (the soul) experiences the vastness of the universe and yet significant, as a part of it, in communion with it. . . . The soul, was created for such experiences."[14] Yet, as Father Benedict Groeschel points out,

> Christian spirituality is not philosophy, scriptural exegesis, theology or liturgy, although all of these may serve to help us relate to the transcendent God. Christian spirituality is a personal relationship with the living Christ and, through Him, with the Father and the Holy Spirit. This is Christian transcendence. It is in every sense of the word *personal*, as is seen in the lives of such fervent Christians as Saint Stephen, who called out in his martyrdom to the living Christ.[15]

Jesuit Father George Aschenbrenner describes the transformation this relationship brings about: "Gradually more and more identified in God's love alone, the priest experiences a certain disengagement from the world as an identity center—precisely because he is so fully engaged with the fire of God's love."[16]

The dearth of vocations to the priesthood is due to a dearth of challenge. For the challenge to be recognized, it must be heard in a personal way from the person who issued it. The challenge is provided by the Gospel radicalism of following Jesus Christ. Sounds simple, doesn't it? Yet the most personal way to follow Jesus Christ is by being vulnerable (*vulnera*, Latin for "wounds"), by entering into His body through His wounds, in an act of self-surrender which is an act of love towards God and neighbor. Entrance into

His body is an entrance into a relationship with all the members of His Body, especially the most wounded and suffering ones; the entrance into His body participates intimately in His personal interiority by participating in His prayer.[17]

We have repeatedly spoken of the highest human capacity, which is to give oneself in love. This involves a self-emptying, a *kenosis*, by which we share in the kenosis of Christ in self-emptying love. This entrance into the body of Christ through His wounds can only take place in response to His personal call. To recognize that this call has come from the Lord is to know that my love is radically more than my own initiative and will need to be sustained by more than my own efforts; rather, what is called for is the total *emptying* of self, which can only take place in the kenosis of Jesus Christ, who calls us to take up our cross and *follow Him.* Secondly, this call means a radical, total gift of self, not a negotiated investment that can be calculated and measured. Thirdly, the commitment is a personal one, made in a radically personal way, to and through Jesus Christ to His Church, the members of His Body. This call is issued to any one who follows Jesus Christ; if one is called to follow in an undivided way, how much more intimately must that one by absorbed into His wounds?

The Evangelical Counsels

In his classic work *Priest and Bishop,* Sulpician Father Raymond Brown asserts that the Church has every right to ask her priesthood to ground and root itself in the life of discipleship presented in the Gospels. This means that priestly life cannot be reduced to an understanding of priesthood seen simply as a solution created by the Church herself but rather as a gift from her Lord,[18] a gift that can only be understood in light of the evangelical counsels. There are many spiritual deficits accruing from the tendency to see the evangelical counsels as the province of those with a religious vocation and not as pertinent to the secular or diocesan priesthood. Cardinal Hans Urs von Balthasar believes that the development of a spirituality of a secular or diocesan priesthood separate from explicit reference to the evangelical counsels is to be understood as a concession on the part of the Church—a concession which leaves obedience stripped of all but a canonical relationship with an ordinary, diminishes poverty to a vague ideal that does not even merit a mention in the liturgy of ordination, and reduces chastity to a promise of celibacy.[19] To be called into the priesthood of Christ is to be a priest who is himself the victim, in imitation of Christ, both Priest and Victim. We have already noted the teaching of the Second Vatican Council, elaborated in the *Directory for the Life and Ministry of Priests*, that the priest is a man of communion: this *communio* is formed within Christ's gift of Himself, and can only be maintained as a synthesis of kenosis, love, and ecclesial life.[20] The "I" of the priest becomes the "I" of Christ's mission, so that with Saint Paul the priest can no longer say "I" in reference to himself alone, but also to Christ who lives in him (Gal. 2:20) and the Church for whose sake he lives (Phil. 1:23–25).

Where can we find an example of this ideal? The patron of parish priests is Saint John Vianney, yet Thomas O'Meara in his book *The Theology of Ministry* suggests that the Curè of Ars is an inadequate model of priesthood in light of needs for ministry in our times.[21] But in fact, the priestly ministry of the Curè of Ars included all the essential dimensions of priesthood: the sacramental, especially the Eucharist and Reconciliation, the ministry of the Word, and the ministry to the sick, all performed in a radical way. His days spent in the church celebrating Mass and hearing confessions, his constant visits to the sick, his long nights praying and writing his homilies while battling the devil—these are all elements of a parish priestly life being lived radically. Truly, Saint John Vianney lived his priestly life with an ever-expanding priestly heart. In his catechetical instruction, he writes:

> Prayer is nothing but union with God. When one has a heart that is pure and united with God, he is given a kind of serenity and sweetness that makes him ecstatic, a light that surrounds him with marvelous brightness. In this intimate union, God and the

soul are fused together like two bits of wax that no one can ever
pull apart. My little children, your hearts are small, but prayer
stretches them and makes them capable of loving God.[22]

Is it any wonder that his priestly ministry came to be distin-
guished by so many extraordinary charisms and by his personal
holiness? The story is told that Saint John Vianney became lost on
his way to his new assignment at the parish in Ars, and when ask-
ing a little boy the way to the village said, "You show me how to
get to Ars, and I'll spend the rest of my life showing Ars how to get
to heaven. . . . Give me souls—keep all the rest. If a priest has died
as a result of trial and trouble undergone for the glory of God and
the salvation of souls, that would not be such a bad thing."[23]

The priestly life of Saint John Vianney was a life lived according to the evangelical counsels. Vatican Council II speaks of these
counsels as an intensification of the baptismal character of the
people of God, and they are thus to be identified not only with a
vowed religious life but with every Christian life, and most surely
with one who is seeking in an undivided way to lead a religious life
in ordained ministry. Indeed, the ordained priest, within the
liturgy of the sacrament of Holy Orders, promises obedience to
his ordinary and celibacy for life; it is not possible to live the life
of ordained priesthood in a radical way without also living in some
separation from the world. This led Cardinal Balthasar to see
ordained priesthood as occupying a medial position between the
lay state and consecrated religious life.[24]

In our times, there is a great preoccupation with self-realization
and personal fulfillment. Now priestly assignments are usually
given only after extensive consultation, and are only accepted after
the new pastor has a chance to visit the new place to see if he likes
the location and the condition of the facilities, to check the books
and decide whether his dog is going to like it there. Many times
in the past and in the present, priests have felt abused and abandoned by their bishop and the Church when they were forced to
accept difficult assignments while others were given the "breaks."

In this climate, talk of obedience can become meaningless. Many priests feel quite entitled to threaten that they will take an early retirement and live in the house they have bought, or incardinate in some other diocese.

And there is much in priestly life that just seems unfair. Nowadays, it is important to priests to know that they have been heard when they have brought some important aspect of their life and ministry to their bishop's attention, especially when a new assignment is being considered. A priest should feel he is being listened to even if at the end of the discussion he is still asked to take an unwanted assignment, or to move when he does not feel ready. But what is essential is for priestly spirituality to be strengthened by making robust sacrifices, not grudgingly but out of love, to obey in the faith that God's loving providence is at work in mysterious, hidden ways and writes straight even on the crooked lines of political machinations and bureaucratic indifference.

Obedience is a promise made by an ordained priest in a way that should encompass his whole life, grounding it in an act of faith that the Lord will respond to the total gift of oneself, which includes even the surrender of personal choice and freedom. Obedience should not be abandoned when I am not able at the outset to see what good it will bring about, or when it becomes evident that being obedient is not resulting in my living in the best of all possible worlds. Obedience is meant to be an act of total reliance on the Lord, grounded in a hearty faith and in the fruitfulness of sacrifice and self-gift. Its observance should never be contingent on whether others are doing so or come from the expectation that there will be some tradeoff or payback later because they will know, and I will never forget, that "they owe me one."

The truth is that we will never fulfill ourselves. We are, each one of us, a bottomless pit. The only way to become full is to empty oneself of everything. When Simon's name was changed to Peter, and Saul's to Paul, this was an expression that each was no longer a private person but would now speak in the "ecclesial I." There is indeed a sacrifice of self in this self-emptying love; yet for the one so chosen and called, the priestly life provides the greatest opportunity to pursue the call in its fullness, as the only hope of expressing the inner core of himself in the most profoundly intimate way. The assimilation of his personal identity to the identity of Christ is the only way that one who is truly called to be a priest can find peace and allow what is most distinctive and personal in himself to grow to its greatest fullness.[25]

The kenosis of Christ was an act of total obedience. In this is a submission made in love, and made in the heart of the love of Christ obedient to His Father. Obedience cannot be partial, now or then, or only on my own terms. Ultimately, it must be more than merely an offering of all that I have—it must be an offering of my very self. By virtue of this radical commitment, an exclusive dedication to his priestly life and ministry is required of the priest. The disciples left their nets and were told, "Henceforth you will be catching men" (Lk. 5:10). Saint Paul continued to work as a tentmaker so that he would not burden the community, but went on to ask, "Is it only Barnabas and I who have no right to refrain from working?" (1 Cor. 9:6). Vatican Council II allows for the engagement of a priest in secular activities and at times even to attend to a secular profession, but this is occasional, and must never take away from the sacred ministry (LG 31). Surely in our own times the need for priests wholly dedicated to the apostolate is obvious. Even beyond exigencies of circumstance, there is the need for radical and total commitment as self-gift.

Priestly Prayer

While rightly criticizing seminaries for failing to provide formation for living celibacy, Richard Sipe describes the ongoing integration of celibacy and sexuality:

There is *no* possibility of participating seriously in the celibate process or any hope of achieving celibacy without a solid grounding in prayer. That reality is as simple and irreducible as the fact that a human being cannot live without air or water. To phrase it affirmatively, celibacy requires a foundation of prayer. . . . Yet like everyone else, the celibate should be free to choose and explore his or her own method of prayer. Those of us who are called to religious celibate dedication, but who seek sexual integration, also need prayer. Think about it. Prayer is the one place in time when we can be our real selves. . . . Prayer, whatever the method, is the absence of posturing. Prayer means facing ourselves as we really are in the safety and privacy of our hearts. . . . Prayer or its equivalent . . . is a component of sexual integration and love.[26]

There are of course the tired excuses that amount to excusing a priest from ever really setting aside any undivided time for prayer: "My work is my prayer," "I have no time for prayer," "If I am supposed to pray that much I should have been a monk," "I either get too distracted or just fall asleep." While we heartily praise the prayer intermittently uttered in the midst of a busy schedule and especially in moments of need, the quick visits to the Blessed Sacrament, and the snatches of time taken to scan a commentary on the Scriptures to come up with a homily, all these together and by themselves are simply not enough. It is necessary on a daily basis to spend prolonged quality time in prayerful communion with the Lord. Spiritual reading, thinking about God or about life, sitting quietly and reflecting—all of these are valuable, but in themselves they are not yet prayer.

As Pope Benedict XVI points out, according to the testimony of Sacred Scripture, the center of the life and person of Jesus is His constant communion with His Father, that is, His prayer.[27] Not only is Jesus presented as frequently withdrawing into loving, prayerful communion with His Father, often throughout the night and particularly while making important discernment (cf. Mk. 1:35, 6:46, 14:35), but the core of the very personality and identity of Jesus is His relationship of constant communication with the Father as the Son: "The Christian confession is not a neutral proposition; it is prayer, only yielding its meaning within prayer . . . ; only by entering into Jesus' solitude, only by participating in what is most personal to him, his communication with the Father, can one see what this most personal reality is."[28]

The *Abba* of Jesus, the beloved Father of this beloved Son, is shared with us who dare, only through the Son, to call him *our* Father. How can one who would live as *alter Christus*, as another Christ, fail to do otherwise? It is essential for a priest, and the more active he is the more essential it is, to develop an unceasing prayer, nourished by prolonged periods of time each day spent in prayer of praise and petition, in prayer of speaking but also of listening, in prayer of wordless communion. This prolonged time of prayer is the proverbial "holy hour," and many of us have found it necessary to spend this time the first hour we are awake because every hour after that becomes too unpredictable. This extended time spent in communion with the Lord can then be reinforced by those shorter times of prayer throughout the day: the Liturgy of the Hours, the decade of the Rosary prayed while driving to the hospital or walking to the parish center for a meeting.

All this is not undertaken merely as an attempt to force a peace of mind or a less stress-filled disposition. The unceasing prayer of which we speak is the living water Jesus promised to the Samaritan woman; it is the peace He wished for His disciples, as His legacy to them in His Passion, death, and Resurrection. It may be necessary for overachieving workaholic priests to remember again and again that prayer is not an accomplishment but a grace, meaning that it is a free gift. And we enter it through the wounds of Christ, so that we can be Him for those members of His Body who are most wounded, whether they know it or not. This is the fulfillment of the nuptiality of our humanity, and we have seen that the vulnerability of the intimate self-gift we become is the vulnerability of the *vulnera,* of the wounds of Christ. My own wounds best attune me to these points of entry into prayerful communion with Christ and into representing Him, making Him present in kenotic service and ministry to the members of His flock.

Eucharistic Prayer and Reconciliation

Ultimately, Jesus died praying. At the Last Supper, He antici-
pated His death and gave of Himself, so that on the Cross He
might give Himself as an act of prayer, of worship, of glory, and
ultimately, as an act of love.[29] This indissoluble bond between the
Last Supper and the death of Jesus changes death, which is the end
of every earthly communication, into an act of self-communica-
tion in which life triumphs over death.[30] And this act of self-
communication is His holy communion with us, the Eucharistic
communion which must be the center of the life of everyone
who follows Christ and especially of one who represents Him in
making Him present in the Eucharist. "Where two or more are
gathered in my name, there am I in their midst" (Mt. 8:20). Yet
the ordained priest makes Christ present in a unique, sacramental
way. The Blessed Sacrament is the embodiment of Christ's total
self-gift in love, the sacrament of His kenosis, the sacrament of His
vulnerability to the point of death, the sacrament of entry into His
wounds by participating in Christ's own prayer. Is this not precisely what the ordained priest does in the Eucharistic prayer when
he speaks in the words, in the very prayer of Christ: "This is my
body given up for you," "This is my blood," "Do this in memory
of me," "I absolve you of all your sins." The priest speaks these
words of Christ as a memorial that makes this mystery of faith
real, so that all of us might enter into this mystery and become one
with all others by becoming one with Him. All the members of
the Body of Christ are privileged to receive in the Eucharist His
very Body and Blood into our own body and blood, so as to
become one with Him as He becomes one with us. In view of the
reality of this wondrous mystery, is it so hard to believe that, having become one with us, He will give us the gift of unceasing
prayer, of unceasing communion with Him?

The ordained priest must enter into these mysteries, which he
celebrates in an undivided way. This is the reason why a priest celebrates the Eucharist daily; this celebration becomes the heart of
his day because Christ is the heart of his heart. It is also why a pref-

erential way of prayer, of prolonging and deepening this Eucharistic union, is adoration before the Blessed Sacrament. Reserved and even exposed before us, Christ allows His presence to be savored and adored in the most explicit way possible. Personal prayer in thanksgiving upon receiving the Eucharistic Lord or adoring Him in the Blessed Sacrament in solitary prayer does not privatize the Eucharist in a way that competes with Eucharistic table fellowship and service to others, for they are also the broken Body and poured-out Blood of Christ. These two are complementary; neither the communal nor personal dimension of Eucharist can be lost, any more than either the sacramental or interpersonal meanings of Eucharist can cancel each other out.

On October 18, 2002, the Vatican Congregation for the Clergy issued an instruction, "The Priest: Pastor, and Leader of The Parish Community," which prescribes Eucharistic adoration and prayer as the remedy for priestly burnout:

> Spending time in intimate conversation with and adoration of the Good Shepherd, present in the most blessed Sacrament of the altar, is a pastoral priority far superior to any other. . . . Every priest, who is a leader of his community, should attend to this priority so as to ensure that he does not become spiritually barren nor transformed into a dry channel no longer capable of offering anything to anyone . . . any pastoral initiative, missionary program or effort at evangelization that eschews the primacy of spirituality and divine worship is doomed to failure.[31]

A core meaning of Eucharist is forgiveness: "This is the cup of my blood, the blood of the new and everlasting covenant. It will be shed for you and for all, for the forgiveness of sins." To become one with Christ and all the members of His Body requires reconciliation. Here, too, while forgiveness and reconciliation must come to permeate all our lives and relationships, sacramental Reconciliation is a most powerful way of receiving the poured out love of Jesus Christ. Sadly, priests appear to celebrate the sacrament of Reconciliation all too seldom, and perhaps this is a reason for the decline of its practice among all the baptized. Are the casual attitudes of some people toward Eucharistic devotional prayer and to the practice of confession due to casual attitudes found among priests who alone can minister these two sacraments? Is the vulnerability required of both recipient and minister of these sacraments what is being avoided? Or is the intimacy of the relation with Christ in these sacraments that which seems "too good to be true"?

So many elements of the spirituality of ordained priesthood come together in the Eucharist, in the priestly self-gift made in the priestly self-gift of Christ.

> To enter into the service of the Lord means entering into his form of life, a form that exactly and entirely coincides with his service. He gives his flesh and blood for the life of the world. Of course, this is a flesh and blood that cannot be touched directly, one not born of sexual relations or claimed by anyone for a private relationship. Jesus' unmarried state quite explicitly and essentially belongs to his Eucharistic surrender on the Cross.[32]

So also the ordained priest—living celibately, obediently, poorly, prayerfully—seeks to enter ever more deeply into that Eucharistic surrender.

Marian Priestly Spirituality

One can muse on the reasons why priests may need to keep a connection with the feminine through Marian devotion. Some may even suspect there may be in the personal lives of some priests an inability to let go of attachments to their own mothers, or some deep-seated need to idealize her, and all women, in a way that keeps them chaste or on a pedestal. Does the priest who remains the "eternal boy" described by Father Cozzens need to maintain devotion to a glorified queen mother in order to retain his own throne? As interesting as these questions might be, it is just as interesting to see the intense reactions of some, many of them priests, against Marian devotion or the Rosary, as well as other devotions, sacramentals,

and other means of simple faith. Do unresolved personal attachments underlie such attacks upon the piety of others?

The Scriptures do not record Mary's presence at the Last
Supper, where Jesus told His apostles, "Do this in memory of me."
She is, however, present in the upper room at the time of Pentecost,
praying with the apostles as they are filled with the Holy Spirit and
burst forth to preach the Good News (Acts 1:13–14). This is an
extension of the prayerfulness in which Mary is depicted at the
time of her Annunciation, and in which she seems to have abided,
pondering in her heart. Yet this scene where she is pondering and
praying with the disciples, a scene probably recreated by them
many times in the following years, represents what has unfolded in
the life and Tradition of the Church about the unique role of Mary,
Mother of the Church and Mother of priests.

Pope John Paul II in *Gift and Mystery* describes his own early
veneration of Mary:

> At the time when my priestly vocation was developing . . . a
> change took place in my understanding of devotion to the
> Mother of God. . . . At one point I began to question my devo-
> tion to Mary, believing that, if it became too great, it might end
> up compromising the supremacy of the worship owed to Christ.
> At that time I was greatly helped by a book by St. Louis Marie
> Grignion de Montfort, *Treatise of True Devotion to the Blessed
> Virgin.* There I found the answers to my questions. Yes, Mary
> does bring us closer to Christ; she does lead us to him, provided
> we live her mystery in Christ.[33]

Dominican Cardinal Pierre Paul Philippe observes that it was
through Mary that Jesus was made Priest, because it was through
her that He united His divine nature with human nature, thereby
becoming the mediator between God and humanity:

> Jesus did not need a special consecration to become a priest: He
> is the Priest by the sole fact of His Incarnation for He had unit-
> ed within Himself all of Divinity and all of humanity. The Word
> of God, with infinite love, was "precipitated" in the virginal

womb so as to wed humanity and save it. Immediately upon becoming the Son of Mary, the Son of God was made Priest. As the mother of the eternal priest, she is the mother of all priests who derive their priesthood from him. . . . The redemptive sacrifice is a priestly act that Jesus the High Priest offered as He abandoned Himself in a bloody holocaust to the Father. All of this means that Mary was truly and fully our Mother only on Calvary. Like Christ and in union with Him, her loving communion with the divine will would lead her up to Calvary and would be, in that moment, the driving force behind all of her acts. It is only then that she gave us birth into grace.[34]

Personal Honesty and Spiritual Direction

Obviously, there are dangers of self-deception in the spiritual life, dangers by which the priest may be even more threatened because of his status, education, and formation. It goes without saying (so we will say it) that a priest needs to be engaged consistently in a process of spiritual direction. A close friend who knows me may be very helpful, yet it is important to find a director who has enough objectivity to see and tell me the truth. Ongoing education, study, and spiritual reading likewise can challenge me to move beyond what I already know and think—especially what I already know and think about myself. Monsignor Philip Murnion, former director of the National Pastoral Life Center in New York, describes the priest preaching and teaching in his parish as "the church minister who is the primary theologian in the church . . . the theologian on his feet"; he goes on to warn, however, that the priest therefore needs a continually maturing and theologically grounded spirituality. Dean Hoge's research at the Life Cycle Institute of the Catholic University of America shows that priests feel their greatest need is for help in their personal spiritual development.[35]

Many of the elements of priestly spirituality which are means of the most powerful renewal, such as devotion to the Eucharist and devotion to Mary, spiritual direction, and immersion in a deeper life of prayer, can certainly be easily justified theologically

and have been clearly promoted by Vatican II and other magisterial teaching. The same wisdom has been summarized yet again in
the "Concluding Message to all Priests in the World," issued by
the Congregation for the Clergy at the International Symposium
of the Promulgation of the Conciliar Decree *Presbyterorum
Ordinis*. I am not sure whether I am more concerned about how
few priests read these documents or about how easy it can be to
read them and every other thing published on priesthood without
ever undertaking the actual measures that will allow one to under-
go conversion and renewal.

Often priests may have a distaste for certain elements and
practices essential to priestly spirituality, perhaps thinking these
elements are not for them or do not fit their own personal spirituality, and can become locked in powerful resistance. I have
found it most helpful when working with priests and seminarians
in spiritual direction as well as in retreat or formation conferences
to just urge: "Try it. You will see the power of prayer before the
Blessed Sacrament if you simply spend an hour praying there each
day"; "Just try praying the Rosary every day, whether it seems
uplifting or not, even if you haven't done so since you were a boy";
"If you persevere at it, you will see the difference." I have found
that even those skeptical persons, many priests being among them,
who appear to me to have come from Missouri, the "Show me"
state, will find if they persevere even for a relatively short time that
there is simply a power to the sacraments, especially to the
Eucharist and the absolution of sins, as well as to devotion to the
saints and to the Blessed Mother.

Priestly Spirituality: Fraternity and Communion

One of the characteristics of this present generation of seminarians is their enjoyment of the common life in seminary. I can
recall just a decade or two ago when, at the onset of a vacation, the
seminary emptied out so quickly that it was truly astonishing.
Now there is more of a lingering, enjoying the camaraderie and
fraternity as well as the deep and often lasting friendships that are

often formed. Much of this change may come from the reality that many of these men are older and have fewer family and friends at home to whom they can return, but the difference lies deeper than that. There is a much greater appreciation of community life, and a much greater desire to find it in rectory and parish existence when they are ordained.

We have passed through a couple of decades where ongoing priestly formation and renewal programs have abounded, along with various attempts to form clergy support groups and other forms of priestly fellowship. Many of these efforts have borne much fruit, combining various recipes of prayer, recreation, study, and supportive sharing. We have also mentioned the need for mentoring especially of the newly ordained but also of those who are new pastors or changing ministry in some way or another. How can a priest build a community in his parochial setting if he is not himself a man of community, a man of communion?

Once again, we reiterate that there is no mutual exclusiveness between the personal prayer and individual life of a priest and the common prayer and fraternal dimension of the priesthood. The practice of praying the Liturgy of the Hours, the prayer of the Church, a canonical requirement for all those in orders, reflects this perfectly. First, there has been an attempt to provide opportunities for priests to pray the Liturgy of the Hours together as well as a revival of the practice of praying this prayer of the Church in parishes on a regular basis. Secondly, and most importantly, this prayer can be an invisible but very real act in union with all those others, and especially all other priests, who are also praying these prayers. Some priests have abandoned the practice of praying their office because it seems to be such a lonely, routine chore. It should be precisely the opposite, since it is, like all prayer, an act in solidarity with the whole Church.

Priestly fraternity requires hard work, as does any other important dimension of human life. Many priests become isolated as they become overworked. The present shortage of priestly vocations does not help the matter any. There is also a great need for renewal of the fraternity among priests, especially within each particular presbyterate. Most priests will readily admit that there is an intimacy unique to relationships and friendships with other priests. It is tragic when gatherings of priests become gripe sessions and have other destructive consequences, causing some priests to become demoralized and begin to avoid them. There is often a disconnection from the special relationship priests should have with their bishop and with each other around their bishop. When these relationships are deficient, then the whole understanding of Church becomes confused and a priest has less and less to give his people. Yet when these relationships are in place, there is an intimacy and spiritual strength among priests beyond any comparison.

The priest is a man of communion because he is one who is sent to all the people. The priesthood should never become elitist or be lived out in a fraternity with one's fellow priests as if they all belong to the same exclusive country club. Instead, priestly fraternity should make one more ready to be sent, more ready to give oneself to the flock with which one has been entrusted. A priest who is a man of communion does not hide in his office any more than he hides in his bedroom. He does not hide behind his desk or his computer anymore than he hides in the sacristy or behind ritual. He must be radically vulnerable to those with whom he has entered into self-giving communion, and he will never burn out in doing so because he will always realize that when he gives himself totally the Lord is always replenishing the supply. When the disciples wanted to send the hungry crowd home because they only had a few loaves and fishes with which to feed them, Jesus still said, "They need not go away; you give them something" (Mt. 14:16; Mk. 6:37; Lk. 9:13). If we let the Lord bless the little we think we have and break it up and pass it out, we will have more leftover than we started with. If we are giving of our time and energy in a calculating way, as if it is *our* time and *our* energy, we will always be running out. As Mother Teresa consoled Father Benedict Groeschel when he and his little band were undertaking their new foundation among the poor of the South Bronx with very little money in their pockets: "Don't worry, God has lots of money!" God also has all the time and energy we will ever need because He is the source of all time and energy. I will always be running out if I act like my time, my energy, my gifts, my faith, my vocation, my love are actually mine.

As men of communion, priests must always be striving to reach out more to all those to whom they have been sent. Following the example of Jesus, this means seeking out the lost sheep. We must recognize as the lost or forgotten ones those who have no one to shepherd them, and a good way to identify these ones among my flock is to look for the ones I might not want to minister to. A priest cannot say "I hate kids" or " I don't do hospitals." If I feel that way, I probably need, at least for a while, to give pride of place to that particular part of the flock I shepherd. Even more importantly, I need to be certain, as Jesus admonished, not to pay special attention only to the people who can pay me back, such as those who are well placed in terms of means and power, those with whom I have some affinity and whom I feel I understand, or those who I know will thank me or appreciate me. It is necessary to go out first to the ones who may not thank or appreciate me, who will never pay me back, and to whom it may never occur that they should even try.

It may seem like the Good Shepherd was foolish to leave the other ninety-nine to go after the single lost sheep, or that the prodigal father was neglecting his faithful son by fussing so much over the unfaithful one. Likewise, most priests experience a continual reaction from various ones among the flock who feel neglected, and they are usually the very ones who actually consume the most time. But God loves each one as if he were the only person in the world. Somehow, each of the one hundred sheep were being loved and cared for by the Good Shepherd as if each of them were the only one, which is why He left the other ninety-nine in search of the one that was lost; and this is the way a priest who shepherds in His name must also be. If that sounds impossible, remember, God has lots of love and care!

The Reason for the Hope

As these reflections should be making obvious, there is a tremendous need for radical renewal in priestly life and for the kind of vision and leadership that makes a difference in the way in which priests are truly men of communion, meeting and supporting each other in priesthood and ministry and giving of themselves totally to those to whom they have been sent. The reform of the priesthood, which is needed badly at this time, will come as it always has in the course of the history of the Church: from holy persons who live their vocation radically, in a way that inspires and transforms their fellow priests. The only way for this ongoing renewal to take place and for the greatest support to be extended to other priests is for each one to actually live the priestly life as a total gift of self. It will be necessary in our own times, as it has been throughout the history of the Church, for courageous reformers to arise whose least concern is drawing attention to themselves, but who by their own lives will inspire their brother priests to conversion and holiness. I have come to the conclusion, based not only on Church history or my experience working with seminarians and priests or with my spiritual directees but based fundamentally upon my own sorry struggle with conversion, that reform just does not take place unless it is radical, unless it is total, unless it is grounded in the person of Jesus Christ. Jesus' office as shepherd and priest has been handed on and reproduced by Himself, starting with His paradoxical question to Saint Peter by Lake Tiberias: Do you love me more than these?" Cardinal Balthasar reflects further:

> If the subjective assimilation to the attitude of the Good Shepherd lies in Peter's confession of love, its objective status lies in Jesus' promise to him that he will be martyred. . . . That Peter will be led where he "would not go" does not contradict this. It only means that death by martyrdom does not correspond to the will of human nature, just as Jesus did not spontaneously desire to be crucified: "Not my will, but thine be done." This scene by the lake concludes with "Follow me."[36]

Accepting this invitation requires a heart centered on Jesus, an ever-expanding heart being poured out in the very self-outpouring of Jesus. Such a heart is undivided though it is already broken, given to Christ alone so as to be given through Him to everyone else. The face of the priesthood may change superficially, but its heart never will—for the only heart of the priesthood is the unchanging heart of Jesus Christ.

Notes

Preface

[1] Cardinal Avery Dulles, SJ, *The Priestly Office: A Theological Reflection* (Mahwah, NJ: Paulist Press, 1997), 3.

[2] Bishop Boyea's article, "Another Face of the Priesthood," states: "Fr. Cozzens frankly acknowledges that his book is impressionistic." In his preface to *The Changing Face of the Priesthood*, Father Cozzens writes that his reflection, "is grounded in and shaped by my own experience as a priest. . . . The experiences and reflections of many priests, I am sure, will lead them to see a different picture than the one I outline in the pages ahead.'" Bishop Boyea's article is well worth reading in its entirety. *First Things*, no. 110 (February 2001): 31–34, www.firstthings.com/ftissues/ft0102/articles/boyea.html.

[3] Archbishop Timothy M. Dolan, *Priests for the Third Millennium* (Huntington, IN: Our Sunday Visitor, 2001); George Weigel, *The Courage to Be Catholic: Crisis, Reform, and the Future of the Church* (New York: Basic Books, 2002); Benedict Groeschel, CFR, *From Scandal to Hope* (Huntington, IN: Our Sunday Visitor, 2002).

Chapter One

[1] Cf. Donald B. Cozzens, *The Changing Face of the Priesthood: A Reflection on the Priest's Crisis of Soul* (Collegeville: Liturgical Press, 2000), 143.

[2] Dulles, *The Priestly Office.*

[3] Edward Schillebeeckx, *Ministry: Leadership in the Community of Jesus Christ* (New York: Crossroad, 1981), 72–73, 138–39.

[4] See, for example, Michael S. Rose, *Goodbye, Good Men* (Washington: Regency Press, 2002).

[5] Stephen J. Rossetti, *A Tragic Grace: The Catholic Church and Child Sexual Abuse* (Collegeville: Liturgical Press, 1996).

[6] A. W. Richard Sipe, *Celibacy: A Way of Loving, Living, and Serving* (Liguori, MO: Triumph Books, 1996).

[7] Dermot Power, *A Spiritual Theology of the Priesthood: The Mystery of Christ and the Mission of the Priest* (Washington, D.C.: Catholic University of America Press, 1998), 54. See also *Catechism*, nos. 1536–1600.

[8] Jean Galot, SJ, *Theology of the Priesthood* (San Francisco: Ignatius Press, 1985), 22.

[9] Galot, *Theology of the Priesthood*, 32.

[10] Cardinal Hans Urs von Balthasar, "Priestly Existence," in *Explorations in Theology, Vol. II: Spouse of the Word* (San Francisco: Ignatius Press, 1991), 380.

[11] Galot, *Theology of the Priesthood*, 56–57.

[12] Ibid., 58.

[13] Balthasar, *Explorations II*, 380.

[14] Galot, *Theology of the Priesthood*, 94.

[15] Ibid., 45–48.

[15] Ibid., 49, 55.

[17] Ibid., 77.

[18] Ibid., 157, 159.

[19] Ibid., 165.

[20] Ibid., 161.

[21] Clement, as quoted in Galot, *Theology of the Priesthood*, 77, 86, 166.

[22] Ibid., 166.

[23] Balthasar, *Explorations II*, 384, 396, 416.

[24] Dulles, *The Priestly Office*, 9. This point of view is also articulated by Cardinal Hans Urs von Balthasar, who goes so far as to point out that "the Church, which is built 'upon the foundation of the apostles and prophets' (Eph 2:20), was familiar at the beginning, before the apostles laid hands on others, with a celebration of the Eucharist by the 'prophets' who possessed no ordination other than the call by God and were legitimated for this act by their charism; Judas Barsabbas and Silas in the Acts of the Apostles are already examples of this (Acts 13:15f; 15: 22-32), and probably those who spoke tongues and the prophets of Corinth (I Cor 14:16), and in any case the 'prophets and teachers' of the *Didache* (11:3f), who are those with the vocation to celebrate the liturgy in that book-ordained bishops and deacons are 'also' to be admitted to celebrate the liturgy in addition to them. Odo Casel demonstrates that in I Corinthians 12:28 and Ephesians 4:11 'apostles, then prophets, then teachers' are the members of the original charismatic hierarchy that was still at this stage instituted by God and is only abrogated by the ordination carried out by the apostles, while appearing, in the consciousness of the Fathers, as something that has not been totally abolished; thus in the *Canons of Hippolytus* (6:43f), where martyrs need no further human ordination because they 'have attained the spirit of the priesthood' through their confession, and where the case of a confessor who had not been tortured, while the ordination was to be carried out, that part of the ordination prayer which called down upon him the Holy Spirit was to be omitted. Similar texts are found also in several letters of Cyprian (letters 38, 39, 40)." Balthasar, *Explorations II*, 390–91.

[25] Balthasar, *Explorations II*, 391, emphasis omitted.

[26] Clement, as quoted in Galot, *Theology of the Priesthood*, 98.

[27] Ibid., 168.

[28] Clement, as quoted in Raymond E. Brown, *The Critical Meaning of the Bible* (New York: Paulist Press, 1981), 102–3.

[29] H. M. Legrand, "The Presidency of the Eucharist according to the Ancient Tradition," *Worship* 53 (1979): 413–38, as cited in Brown, *Critical Meaning*, 103.

[30] Ignatius of Antioch, *Letter to the Philadelphians* 4.1, as quoted in Galot, *Theology of the Priesthood*, 168.

[31] Hippolytus, as quoted in Dulles, *The Priestly Office,* 9–10.

[32] Christian Cochini, SJ, *The Apostolic Origins of Priestly Celibacy* (San Francisco: Ignatius Press, 1990), 432.

[33] Brown, *Critical Meaning,* 103.

[34] Cf. Cochini, *Apostolic Origins,* 432.

[35] Galot, *Theology of the Priesthood,* 38–39.

[36] Ibid., 197.

[37] Dulles, *Priestly Office,* 11–12.

[38] Galot, *Theology of the Priesthood,* 197.

[39] Pope John Paul II, Post-Synodal Apostolic Exhortation on the Formation of Priests *Pastores Dabo Vobis* (March 25, 1992), no. 11 (hereafter cited in text as PDV).

[40] Pope John Paul II, *Gift and Mystery: On the Fiftieth Anniversary of My Priestly Ordination* (New York: Doubleday, 1996), 44.

[41] Galot, *Theology of the Priesthood,* 203–4.

[42] Ibid., 207.

[43] Mark O'Keefe, OSB, *In Persona Christi: Reflections on Priestly Identity and Holiness* (St. Meinrad: Abbey Press, 1998), 18.

[44] Archbishop Daniel M. Buechlein, "The Sacramental Identity of the Ministerial Priesthood: 'In Persona Christi,'" National Conference of Catholic Bishops, in *Priests for a New Millennium: A Series of Essays on the Ministerial Priesthood* (Washington, D.C.: Secretariat for Priestly Life and Ministry, USCCB, 2000), 44.

[45] Archbishop Daniel Pilarczyk, Address to the Synod of Bishops (Rome, 1990), as cited in Dulles, *The Priestly Office,* 14.

[46] Galot, *Theology of the Priesthood,* 198.

[47] Cf. ibid., 42, 72.

[48] Power, *Spiritual Theology,* 141.

[49] Cf. Galot, *Theology of the Priesthood,* 85.

[50] Cf. Cozzens, *Changing Face,* 5–7.

[51] See Congregation for the Clergy, *Directory on the Ministry and Life of Priests* (Vatican City: Libreria Editrice Vaticana, 1994), 22–23.

[52] Cf. Sipe, *Celibacy,* 86–87.

[53] Cf. Paul Philibert, OP, "Issues for a Theology of Priesthood: A Status Report," in *The Theology of the Priesthood,* eds. Donald J. Goergen and Ann Garrido (Collegeville: Liturgical Press, 2000), 17, 29–36. In response to the debate presented by Father Paul Philibert, I assert that the priest acts *in persona Christi capitis et membra* in a way that is also pneumatological as well as christological, both descending and ascending, in a representation that is direct and real of the *Totus Christus* who embodies the Church. The unique ontological configuration of the priest to Christ is reflected in his moving from

first person plural to first person singular in the words of consecration. As Father Benedict Ashley, OP, points out in his article in the same volume, "Priests act *in persona ecclesiae* only because they act *in persona Christi capitis*." "The Priesthood of Christ, the Baptized and Ordained," in *The Theology of the Priesthood*, eds. Donald J. Goergen and Ann Garrido (Collegeville: Liturgical Press), 164.

[54] Congregation for the Clergy, *Directory*, 12.

[55] Mark O'Keefe, OSB, *The Ordination of a Priest*, (St. Meinrad, In: Abbey Press, 1999), 31.

[56] Pope Pius XII, Encyclical on the Sacred Liturgy *Mediator Dei* (November 20, 1947), no. 69, as cited in Dulles, *The Priestly Office*, 39.

Chapter Two

[1] Galot, *Theology of the Priesthood*, 43.

[2] Cozzens, *Changing Face*, 5.

[3] Thomas P. Rausch, "Priestly Identity: Priority of Representation and the Iconic Argument," *Worship* 73 (1999): 169–79, as cited in Cozzens, *Changing Face*, 5.

[4] Cozzens, *Changing Face*, 5, 8, emphasis in original.

[5] Ibid., 10.

[6] Ibid., 11.

[7] Ibid., 11–12.

[8] Ibid., 12–13.

[9] Power, *Spiritual Theology*, 57, 62.

[10] Balthasar, *Explorations II*, 394.

[11] Cf. Second Vatican Council, Decree on the Pastoral Office of Bishops in the Church *Christus Dominus* (October 28, 1965), no. 28; Second Vatican Council, Decree on the Church's Missionary Activity *Ad Gentes Divinitus* (December 7, 1965), no. 19.

[12] Congregation for the Clergy, *Directory*, no. 16.

[13] See Balthasar, *Explorations II*, 394.

[14] Balthasar, *Explorations II*, 394–95.

[15] Congregation for the Clergy, *Directory*, 19–22.

[16] Ibid., 18.

[17] Ibid., 25–26.

[18] Balthasar, *Explorations II*, 408.

[19] Cozzens, *Changing Face*, 119.

[20] Ibid., 120.

[21] Cf. Bishop Donald W. Wuerl, "The Role of Priests in Catechesis in the New Millennium: Anchored in Tradition," in National Conference of Catholic Bishops,

Priests for a New Millennium: A Series of Essays on the Ministerial Priesthood (Washington, D.C.: Secretariat for Priestly Life and Ministry, USCCB, 2000), 113–126.

[22] Sipe, *Celibacy*, 98.

[23] Ibid., 98.

[24] The archetypal psychological tendency to try to preserve a properly balanced relationship between a dyad can be complemented by an object-relations psychoanalytic approach, such as that developed in the British School by Melanie Klein and Donald Winnicott, which recognizes primitive infantile tendencies toward splitting: between the bad mother and the good mother, between the bad father and the good father. Such primitive splitting can live on in relationships with every other object of love and devotion, in an unconscious splitting which bifurcates those who abuse authority from those who give it away—clergy and laity, liberal and conservative, traditional and experimental, those who are on my side from those who are not, the ones who agree from those who do not. It is hard to find communion if one approaches life in this way, except in the ever-elusive dream of a primitive absorption into an undifferentiated union, which is all-consuming because it incorporates by consuming, remaining incapable of communion or of genuine truth.

[25] Cozzens, *Changing Face*, 16–17.

[26] Boyea, "Another Face of the Priesthood," 32.

[27] See Cozzens, *Changing Face*, 17–18.

[28] Hans Urs von Balthasar, *Explorations in Theology, Vol. IV: Spirit and Insititution* (San Francisco: Ignatius Press, 1995), 364–65.

[29] Address of Pope John Paul II to the Cardinals of the United States (April 23, 2002), no. 3.

[30] Ibid., no. 4.

[31] Cozzens, *Changing Face*, 19.

[32] Ibid., 54–61.

[33] Ibid., 57–59.

[34] Bishop Robert N. Lynch, "Collaborators in Ministry: The Bishop and His Priests," in National Conference of Catholic Bishops, *Priests for a New Millennium: A Series of Essays on the Ministerial Priesthood* (Washington, D.C.: Secretariat for Priestly Life and Ministry, USCCB, 2000), 58–59.

[35] Donald B. Cozzens, "Telling the Truth," *The Tablet*, May 8, 2000.

[36] Sipe, *Celibacy*, 77; for further discussion of loneliness in the priesthood, see ibid., 76–85.

[37] Ibid., 79.

[38] Ibid., 80.

[39] Ibid., 81.

[40] Cozzens, *Changing Face*, 76.

[41] Sipe, *Celibacy*, 82–84.

[42] Ibid., 85.

[43] Ibid., 89, 90, emphasis in original.

[44] Balthasar, *Explorations in Theology IV*, 354.

[45] Ibid., 354–55.

[46] Sigmund Freud, "Beyond the Pleasure Principle," vol. XVII of The Standard Edition of the Complete Psychological Works of Sigmund Freud, trans. James Strachey (London: Hogarth Press, 1955).

[47] As cited in Rossetti, *A Tragic Grace*, 11.

[48] Ralph Earle and Gregory Crow, *Lonely All the Time: Recognizing, Understanding, and Overcoming Sex Addiction, for Addicts and Co-dependents* (Phoenix: Tri Star, 1998), 4ff.

[49] Sipe, *Celibacy*, 120.

[50] Ibid., 116.

[51] Rossetti, *A Tragic Grace*, 112.

[52] Cf. John Harvey, OSFS, *The Truth about Homosexuality: The Cry of the Faithful* (San Francisco: Ignatius Press, 1996).

[53] Earle and Crow, *Lonely All the Time*, 24–25.

[54] Patrick Carnes, *Don't Call It Love: Recovery from Sexual Addiction* (New York: Bantam, 1991), 12–24, 143.

[55] Patrick Carnes, *Out of the Shadows: Understanding Sexual Addiction* (Center City: Hazeldon, 1993), 4.

[56] Patrick Carnes, *A Gentle Path through the Twelve Steps: The Classic Guide for All People in the Process of Recovery* (Center City: Hazeldon, 1993).

[57] Carnes, *Don't Call It Love*, 39, 60.

[58] Earle and Crow, *Lonely All the Time*, 23; Elizabeth A. Horst, *Recovering the Lost Self: Shame-Healing for Victims of Clergy Sexual Abuse* (Collegeville: Liturgical Press, 1998).

[59] Carnes, *Out of the Shadows*, 82–85.

[60] Earle and Crow, *Lonely All the Time*, 44.

[61] Carnes, *Don't Call It Love*, 39, 60.

[62] Ibid., 269.

Chapter Three
[1] George Weigel, *Witness to Hope: The Biography of Pope John Paul II* (New York: Harper Collins, 1999), 342.

[2] Pope John Paul II, *The Theology of the Body: Human Love in the Divine Plan* (Boston: Pauline Books & Media, 1997), 30–31.

[3] John Paul II, 33.

[4] Ibid., 34.

[5] Ibid., 43.

[6] Ibid., 36–37.

[7] Ibid., 38.

[8] Ibid., 38–39.

[9] Ibid., 44–45; cf. ibid., 42.

[10] Ibid., 46–47.

[11] Ibid., 47, 49.

[12] Ibid., 50.

[13] Ibid., 49.

[14] See Sipe, *Celibacy*, 89, 90.

[15] John Paul II, *Body*, 53, 54, 55–7.

[16] Ibid., 67, 68–69.

[17] Ibid., 58.

[18] Cf. Ibid., 58–59, 61.

[19] Ibid., 62–3.

[20] Second Vatican Council, Pastoral Constitution on the Church in the Modern World *Gaudium et Spes* (December 7, 1965), no. 14; cf. John Paul II, *Body*, 63.

[21] John Paul II, *Body*, 70.

[22] Ibid., 65.

[23] Luke Timothy Johnson, "A Disembodied 'Theology of the Body,' John Paul II on Love, Sex, and Pleasure," *Commonweal* CXXVIII, no. 2 (January 26, 2001): 16, 17.

[24] John Paul II, *Body*, 65.

[25] Ibid., 74.

[26] Ibid., 66.

[27] Ibid., 76.

[28] Ibid., 79.

[29] Ibid., 80–81.

[30] John Paul II, *Body*, 82.

[31] Ibid., 88–89.

[32] Ibid., 115.

[33] Ibid., 128.

[34] Ibid., 122–23.

[35] Ibid., 126.

[36] Ibid., 151.

[37] Ibid., 136–37.

[38] Ibid., 138–40, 142.

[39] Ibid., 147, 156–57.

[40] Ibid., 166.

[41] Sigmund Freud, *The Ego and the Id*, vol. 19 of *The Standard Edition of the Complete Psychological Works of Sigmund Freud*, trans. James Strachey (London: Hogarth Press, 1955).

[42] John Paul II, *Body*, 170–71.

[43] Ibid., 173, 172.

[44] Sipe, *Celibacy*, 67–68.

[45] Ibid., 70; Pope Paul VI called for such an asceticism in *Humanae Vitae*, no. 21, as noted by Pope John Paul II in *Body*, 217.

[46] John Paul II, *Body*, 175–76, 200.

[47] Unfortunately, it is not always easy to get a true picture of these issues, either among seminarians and priests or within society in general. With regard to priests and seminarians, many of the generalizations about priesthood in terms of sexuality and sexual maturity found in books like Father Cozzens' *The Changing Face of the Priesthood* are founded on the dated impressions outlined by agenda-driven commentators such as Holy Cross Father Richard McBrien. The journals given credit for calling to public attention such issues as homosexuality and the priesthood are *Atlantic Monthly*, *Newsweek*, and *National Catholic Reporter*, which often popularize and sensationalize. Among the better-known studies of sexuality that have undertaken a broad survey of sexual attitudes in society in general, we can mention the well-known research and publications of Masters and Johnson (William Masters, Virginia E. Johnson, Robert C. Kolodny, *Masters and Johnson on Sex and Human Loving*, Boston: Little Brown & Company, 1988), as well as the report on sexual behavior of the Kinsey Institute, which bills itself as "America's most trusted authority on sex" and "reveals what you must know to be sexually literate" (June M. Reinishch, *The Kinsey Institute New Report on Sex*, New York: St. Martin's Press, 1990; see the critique of Kinsey found in Judith A. Reisman, Edward W. Eichel, John H. Court, J. Gordon Muir, eds., *Kinsey, Sex, and Fraud: The Indoctrination of a People*, Lafayette: Huntington House, 1990). More recent is the "definitive survey" which promises "the answers at last," called *Sex in America* (Robert T. Michael, John H. Gagnon, Edward O. Laumann, and Gina Kolata, *Sex in America: A*

Definitive Survey, Boston: Warner Books, 1994), attempting to identify the most reliable data about sexuality as it is lived, expressed, and understood in America. This last text was recommended to me as most reliable by Father Stephen Rossetti, president of Saint Luke's Institute in Silver Springs, Maryland, who in a personal communication has indicated that this sociological research probably provides the best data currently available to give some context within which to understand the issues we are considering with regard to priesthood and sexuality.

[48] Michael et al., *Sex in America*, 92.

[49] Ibid., 94, 95–96.

[50] Ibid., 232–33.

[51] Ibid., 237.

[52] Sipe, *Celibacy*, 39.

[53] Ibid., 39. Yet what constitutes a lapse? The gross misinterpretation and misunderstanding of this estimate could have been foreseen in that "practicing celibacy" and "being sexually active" are not clearly defined. Is a lapse into masturbation being sexually active and violating the law of celibacy, or does sexually acting out always involve another person? Clearly for Sipe a lapse is not simply a matter of frequency of incidence, but more a question of incidence of a certain kind of activity or relationship that could be considered as compromising celibacy. It is clear that Sipe does not include autoerotic behavior as a lapse since he does not agree with Church teaching that masturbation is morally wrong (pp. 162–63). Hesitations about Sipe's estimates focus on the source of his data. There is a randomness to his sample which limits his ability to draw conclusions about the mainstream of celibate clergy. If I were to assess the state of mental health in America on the basis of my patient population, I would be generalizing on those who are suffering enough to seek help and on the particular types of people who do seek help from a clinician like myself, who is a male, a Freudian psychoanalyst, and a priest. Sipe pointed out in personal communication with me, however, that only a small percentage of his sample consists in patients, the rest being other celibates encountered in other than a therapeutic setting. Still, Father Stephen Rossetti in personal conversation has asserted that his estimate remains Richard Sipe's own on the basis of his experience, which has no way of being verified, and that his sample clearly is not random.

[54] Ibid., 51.

[55] Michael et al., *Sex in America*, 105.

[56] Ibid., 104, 239–41.

[57] Ibid., 100.

[58] "Many Ex-Priests Come Back," *National Catholic Register* 76, no. 48, November 26–December 2, 2000, 1.

[59] Ibid., 7.

[60] Ibid.

[61] Dolan, *Priests for the Third Millennium*, 317.

Chapter Four

[1] Philip Jenkins, "The Myth of the 'Pedophile Priest,'" *Pittsburgh Post-Gazette*, March 3, 2002, C 1, 4.

[2] See Groeschel, *From Scandal to Hope*.

[3] Philip Lawler, "Whose Responsibility," *Catholic World Report* 12, no. 7 (July 2002): 39.

[4] Chelsea J. Carter, "Teacher Sex Cases Overshadowed by Clergy Scandal," *The Bradford (PA) Era*, June 10, 2002, 5.

[5] As Father Benedict Groeschel writes in the *National Review*, "Thirty years ago, no one knew much about pedophilia. In my ten-year training as a psychologist, I never heard pedophilia mentioned once. [Father Groeschel earned his doctorate at Columbia University in New York.] When the cases emerged therapists believed without sufficient evidence that pedophilia could be cured. Dedicated and believing clergy worked with them using spiritual remedies from the sacraments to thirty-day retreats. Time has proven that like most addictions this pathology can only be arrested and not cured" (February 28, 2002).

[6] Richard B. Gartner, *Betrayed as Boys* (New York: Guilford Press, 1999), 99. Gartner asserts that most acts of molestation of children are heterosexual rather than homosexual, and that even among male same-sex abusers there is often a heterosexual interest in children that really involves an attraction to the feminine characteristics of prepubescent boys. As far as the incidence of sexual abuse of minors among priests, Dr. Thomas Drummond asserts that one would not find in adjudicated cases any preponderance of clergy and religious among convicted sexual offenders. "Perpetrators of sexual crimes against minors, and others, come from both genders, all sexual orientations, all professions and strata of society, from celibates and non-celibates alike. . . . Judges, teachers and housewives have all been found to be sex abusers of children and adolescents" ("The Fundamental Problem Underlying Sexual Abuse: A Broken Contract," in *Newsletter of the New Life Institute for Human Development* 10, no. 2 [Spring 2002], 1). For more on the taboo of discussing the sexual abuse of children by women, see Michelle Elliott, *Female Sexual Abuse of Children* (New York: Guilford Press, 1993).

[7] Rossetti, *A Tragic Grace*, 88.

[8] As cited in Rosetti, *A Tragic Grace*, 65, 91.

[9] Ibid., 94–96.

[10] George Weigel, "Church Must Become More Catholic Not Less," *Pittsburgh Catholic*, May 17, 2002.

[11] The data provided in *Sex in America* indicates that 4 percent of women and 6 percent of men indicated that they were (presumably predominantly) attracted to members of the same sex, and that 4 percent of women and 6 percent of men indicated that they have had sex with someone of the same sex at least once (pp. 174–75). Considering a number of other estimates, it would seem reasonable to propose that between 4 and 7 percent of males experience a predominantly same-sex attraction. Among priests and seminarians, it is surely higher. I would reject the higher estimate of 50 or even 80 percent and would estimate that among priests and seminarians less than one-third of that percentage experience a predominantly same-sex attraction.

[12] Stephen J. Rossetti, "The Catholic Church and Child Sexual Abuse," *America* 186, no. 13 (April 22, 2002): 11.

[13] See Rose, *Goodbye, Good Men.*

[14] Brian Caulfield, "Homosexuals Who Change: Psychology's Dogma Breaking Down," *National Catholic Register* 78, no. 28, July 14–20, 2002.

[15] See "Homosexuality and Hope: A Statement of the Catholic Medical Association," http://www.cathmed.org/publications/homosexuality.html, which includes an excellent bibliography; also see "An Open Letter to Bishops," http://www.cathmed.org/publications/openletter.html.

[16] American Psychiatric Association, *Diagnostic and Statistical Manual of Mental Disorders*, 3rd ed. (1980), 380, as cited in Harvey, *The Truth about Homosexuality*, 63.

[17] See Gerald D. Coleman, SS, *Homosexuality: Catholic Teaching and Pastoral Practice* (New York: Paulist Press, 1995), 24.

[18] Kenneth Lewes, *Psychoanalysis and Male Homosexuality* (London: Jason Aronson, 1995), 172, xi–iv.

[19] Susan C. Vaughan, *The American Psychoanalyst* 34, no. 4 (2000): 34.

[20] Sigmund Freud, "Civilized Sexual Morality and Modern Nervous Illness," *Standard Edition* IX, 177–204. Classical psychoanalytic theory inspired by Freud has generally assumed a process more complex than a primary heterosexuality that becomes inhibited and develops homosexually. Rather, the starting point for Freud is a polymorphous development of a primary bisexuality that usually achieves a heterosexual resolution through an inhibition of the homosexual possibility as well as a whole host of other possible oral, anal, and phallic fixations. When heterosexuality is inhibited and the homosexual possibility lies open, an inversion of sexuality takes place and the homosexual preference becomes fixed. The inversion of sexuality found in homosexuality is contrasted by Freud with the perversions established by fixations at other stages of polymorphous psychosexuality, such as the anal and oral ones. Freud's various proposals about the psychodynamics of a homosexual orientation involve the well-known oedipal complex and hypothesis that the young male struggles with castration anxiety both because of his erotic strivings for his mother and the dread of castration coming from the discovery of sexual difference between him and her: the resolution is to revert to a narcissistic object choice, someone like himself who is also the uncastrated mother, the phallic woman. (Sigmund Freud, "Inhibition, Symptoms, and Anxiety," *Standard Edition* XX, 75–176). Thus, homosexuality is one possible resolution to the oedipal complex, attempting to deal with anxiety over castration by a negative oedipal complex by choosing as object of love his father and other males to deal with the threat of castration (Sigmund Freud, "From the History of an Infantile Neurosis," *Standard Edition* XVII, 3–22), and thus every homosexual choice is the rejection of a heterosexual one. There is a regression to earlier phases before the phallic one, and the choice is a narcissistic one, of one like oneself or as one ideally would like to be, resembling the mother and oneself as one must be to be loved by her, resembling someone who was part of oneself and who takes the place of the phallus and assures that the male genitals are there. (Sigmund Freud, "Narcissism: An Introduction," *Standard Edition* XIV, 73–102).

[21] Harvey, *The Truth about Homosexuality*, 158.

[22] See Heinz Kohut, *The Analysis of the Self* (New York: International Universities Press, 1971).

[23] Sigmund Freud, "Mourning and Melancholia," *Standard Edition* XIV, 237–58. Many of these insights into unconscious dynamics of homosexuality that seem self-evident to one who has experience in searching into the unconscious meaning of human desire and love, can seem bizarre speculations and fabrications when they are set forth as we are doing here. Others have also rejected them for other reasons, including many psychoanalysts. It surely is true that Freud's understanding of sexuality is from a masculine, phallocentric point of view, and femininity and female sexuality are basically understood in terms of what is missing from male sexuality. There is a gynecophobia at the heart of the psychoanalytic theory of sexuality (Lewes, *Psychoanalysis and Male Homosexuality*, 226), in that male sexuality, heterosexual or homosexual, is oriented around a fear of the female genitals, and that female sexuality, heterosexual or homosexual, is an ever-unsatisfied attempt to get over what is missing. It goes without saying that female homosexuality and lesbianism have even less of a chance of being analyzed in any illuminating way if female sexuality has not been explored in its own right and richness (see Noreen O'Connor and Loanna Ryan, *Lesbianism and Psychoanalysis: Wild Desires and Mistaken Identities*, New York: Columbia University Press, 1993).

[24] Coleman, *Homosexuality*, 70. The pertinent texts usually cited are: Genesis 19:4–11; Leviticus 18:22, 20:13; Romans 1:26–27; 2 Corinthians 6:9–11; 1 Timothy 1:8–11; and Jude 7. While there is no place in the Bible where homosexual acts are approved, Robin Scroggs has questioned whether Saint Paul is truly condemning all homosexuality in the Letter to the Romans (Rom 1:26–7), since he really is only condemning pederasty (Robin Scroggs, *The New Testament and Homosexuality*, as cited in Harvey, *The Truth About Homosexuality*, 139–40.) Sulpician Father Gerald Coleman, moral theologian and seminary rector, argues that, while Saint Paul is probably only referring to pederasty in this instance, one cannot conclude that he approves other forms of homosexual behavior. Father Coleman also insists that Saint Paul is speaking of "natural" and "unnatural" behavior in a way similar to our use of "deviant," and all of these ideas of Saint Paul must be seen in light of the way in which he upholds marriage as an ideal (Gerald D. Coleman, SS, *Human Sexuality: An All-Embracing Gift*, 254–55, as cited in Harvey, *The Truth about Homosexuality*, 140–41). Professor Daniel Helminiak likewise interprets this text from Saint Paul's Letter to the Romans not as addressing what is unnatural but what is socially unacceptable, and offers an interpretation of some other biblical texts in an attempt to show that they are not really condemning homosexuality: the sin of Sodom is really the sin of inhospitality; the abomination in the book of Leviticus is uncleanness; what is condemned in the First Letter to the Corinthians and the First Letter to Timothy is abusive male-to-male sex. (See Daniel A. Helminiak, *What the Bible Really Says about Homosexuality* [New Mexico: Alamo Press, 2000]). Here, too, I would follow the response of Father Coleman and assert that, whatever the particular sin or abuse being addressed in the Bible, the teaching cannot be restricted to that particular issue such as same-sex abuse, inhospitality or uncleanness, or merely pederasty. The whole biblical context within which the meaning of human sexuality is revealed sees it in light of what sexuality and the body are in light of God's plan. This notion of God's plan grounds our understanding of human nature and of the natural order, and in turn, of what is disordered. The teaching of the Catholic Church is emphatically clear that only homosexual acts and not the orientation itself are sinful.

[25] As cited by Lewes, *Psychoanalysis and Male Homosexuality*, 21–22.

[26] Sigmund Freud, "The Psychogenesis of a Case of Homosexuality in a Woman," vol. 18 of *The Standard Edition of the Complete Psychological Works of Sigmund Freud*, trans. James Strachey, 155–72.

[27] Lewes, *Psychoanalysis and Male Homosexuality*, 54.

[28] Sigmund Freud, "The Psychogenesis of a Case of Homosexuality in a Woman," 155.

[29] Stephen J. Blommer, "Answers to Questions About Sexual Orientation and Homosexuality," as quoted by Dr. Laura Schlessinger in the forward to Richard Cohen, *Coming Out Straight: Understanding and Healing Homosexuality* (Winchester: Oakhill Press, 2000), p. x. See also the article by Brian Caulfield from the *National Catholic Register*, July 14–20, 2002, vol. 78, no. 28, 2, where he mentions a breakthrough article that made its way into a secular and professional journal, *Professional Psychology*, by Professor Warren Throchmorton of Grove City College in Pennsylvania, which asserts regarding eleven studies over a twenty-year period that orientation-change therapy is not harmful.

[30] Joseph Nicolosi, *Reparative Therapy of Male Homosexuality: A New Clinical Approach* (Northvale: Jason Aronson, 1997), 109ff.

[31] Harvey, *The Truth about Homosexuality*, 112.

[32] Gerard J. M. van den Aardweg, *The Battle for Normality: A Guide for Self-Therapy for Homosexuality* (San Francisco: Ignatius Press, 1997), 57, 69–70.

[33] Richard Cohen, *Coming Out Straight*, 25.

[34] Leanne Payne, *Crisis in Masculinity* (Grand Rapids: Baker Books, 1985); Mario Bergner, *Setting Love in Order: Hope and Healing for the Homosexual* (Grand Rapids. Baker Books, 1995).

[35] See the goals of Courage in Harvey, *The Truth about Homosexuality*, 30.

[36] Joe Dallas, *Desires in Conflict: Answering the Struggle for Sexual Identity* (Eugene, OR: Harvest House Publishers, 1991).

[37] Harvey, *The Truth about Homosexuality*, 9, 29.

[38] Elizabeth R. Moberly, *Homosexuality: A New Christian Ethic* (Cambridge: James Clarke & Co., 1983,) 40ff.

[39] Moberly claims that there is a need for a revision of the Church's teaching that the homosexual orientation is not sinful in itself since the homosexual then assumes that God intended him to be as he is, that is, incomplete: "The homosexual condition *as it is* is not 'in the image of God' as is sometimes suggested by homosexuals, but as men and women who are intended to attain psychological maturity in their gender identity. . . . Rather, to seek the will of God in such a situation implies doing all that one can to make good whatever deficits are involved. . . . A non-practicing homosexual is still a homosexual . . . sexual abstinence of itself does not begin to meet the problem of the underlying deficits. Only the nonsexual fulfillment of the same-sex needs may do this (*Homosexuality*, 30, 36, 40).

[40] As reported in the *Pittsburgh Post-Gazette*, May 9, 2001.

[41] Harvey, *The Truth about Homosexuality*, 114.

[42] Ibid., 117.

[43] Aardweg, *The Battle for Normality*, 86–87.

[44] Harvey, *The Truth about Homosexuality*, 19–20, 186.

[45] Schaugnessy, "The Gay Priest Problem," 56.

[46] Harvey suggests a careful process of screening including taking a thorough sexual history during the assessment which they claim can offer a 90 percent accuracy in identifying same-sex attractions, and if necessary, intensive therapy and five years of celibacy before acceptance of candidates who manifest SSA (*The Truth about Homosexuality*, 187, 362–65).

[47] Catholic Medical Association, Letter to the American Bishops (July 23, 2002), http://www.cathmed.org.

[48] Weigel, *The Courage to Be Catholic*, 162–63.

[49] Andrew Greeley, "Bishops Paralyzed Over Heavily Gay Priesthood," *National Catholic Reporter*, November 10, 1989, 13–14, as cited in Cozzens, *Changing Face*, 100–1.

[50] Cozzens, *Changing Face*, 101–2.

[51] Boyea, "Another Face of the Priesthood," 31–34.

[52] I have published some of my assessments elsewhere in "Tomorrow's Priests," *The Priest* 54, no. 12 (December 1998): 41–43.

[53] Greeley, "Bishops Paralyzed Over," 14, as cited in Cozzens, *Changing Face*, 100.

Chapter Five

[1] J. Coppens, "Old Testament Priesthood," in *Priesthood and Celibacy* (Milan, 1972), 13.

[2] Coppens, "Old Testament Priesthood," 16–17, 19–20.

[3] Cf. John Paul II, *Body*, 263.

[4] Balthasar, *Explorations IV*, 392.

[5] John Paul II, *Body*, 269

[6] Cf. ibid., 267.

[7] Ibid., 268.

[8] Ibid., 273.

[9] Ibid., 273, 278.

[10] Ibid., 282–84.

[11] Balthasar, *Explorations IV*, 391.

[12] John Paul II, *Body*, 293.

[13] Ibid., 293–94.

[14] Stefan Heid, *Celibacy in the Early Church: The Beginnings of a Discipline of Obligatory Continence for Clerics in the East and West* (San Francisco: Ignatius Press, 2000), 13, 15.

[15] Heid, *Celibacy in the Early Church*, 13.

[16] Ibid., 311–315.

[17] Thomas McGovern, *Priestly Celibacy Today* (Princeton: Scepter Publishers, 1998), 35.

[18] McGovern, *Priestly Celibacy Today*, 36–37.

[19] Heid, *Celibacy in the Early Church*, 306–11.

[20] Cochini, *Apostolic Origins*, 79–83.

[21] For Tertullian of Carthage, see Heid, *Celibacy in the Early Church*, 72–81; for Clement of Alexandria, see 65–72; for Origen of Alexandria, see 93–105; for Eusebius of Caesarea, see 115–120; for Ephiphanius of Salamis, see 145–49; for Jerome, see 149–52; for John Chrysostom, see 152–56; for Theodore of Mopsuestia, see 159–70; and for others, see 297.

[22] Ibid., 228.

[23] Ibid., 297–305.

[24] A. M. Stickler, "The Evolution of the Discipline of Celibacy in the Western Church from the End of the Patristic Era to the Council of Trent," in *Priesthood and Celibacy*, 582.

[25] Stickler, "The Evolution of the Discipline of Celibacy," 591–92.

[26] Richard Marzheuser, "A New Generation Is on the Rise in Seminaries," in *Seminary Journal*, Fall 1999.

[27] Ibid., 30.

[28] John J. O'Brien, CP, "Intimacy," in *The New Dictionary of Catholic Spirituality*, ed. Michael Downey (Collegeville: Liturgical Press, 1993), 553.

[29] *Webster's Ninth New Collegiate Dictionary*, (1991).

[30] Benedict J. Groeschel, CFR, *Stumbling Blocks or Stepping Stones* (Mahwah, NJ: Paulist Press, 1987), 87.

[31] Keith Clark, "Celibate Life Offers Insights," *Review for Religious* 59, no. 2 (March–April 2000), 137.

[32] Dulles, *The Priestly Office*, 66.

[33] John Paul II, *Body*, 206.

[34] Michael et al., *Sex*, 158.

[35] Sipe, *Celibacy*, 162.

[36] Michael et al., *Sex*, 158–59.

[37] Ibid., 159.

[38] Sipe, *Celibacy*, 163.

[39] Michael et al., *Sex*, 166–67.

[40] Ibid., 167–68.

[41] Ibid., 168.

[42] John Paul II, *Body*, 218–23, 227–28.

[43] Ibid., 238, 241–42, 244.

Chapter Six

[1] "Pope Opens Triduum with Advice for Bishops, Priests," Zenit News Service, April 12, 2001, http://www.zenit.org/english/archive/0104/ZE010412.htm#4590.

[2] Marzheuser, "A New Generation," 27.

[3] Ibid., 27-28, emphasis in original.

[4] Ibid., 29–30.

[5] Ibid., 22.

[6] Ibid., 28–29.

[7] Ibid., 24–25.

[8] Ibid., 29

[9] Ibid., 28.

[10] Paul Shaughnessy, "The Gay Priest Problem," *Catholic World Report* 10, no. 10 (November 2000).

[11] Father Cozzens turns to such luminaries as Father Andrew Greely, Father Richard McBrien, and Father Hans Küng for his understanding of priesthood as well as for the data to help us understand what the problem is. But you can tell a lot about someone by the company they keep, and as Father Benedict Groeschel points out, in Father Cozzens' book there is "no mention at all of saints like Augustine, John Chrysostom, Thomas Aquinas, Alphonsus Ligouri and John Eudes, who wrote extensively on the priesthood. . . . There are only two references, both of them negative, to John Paul II. Although the Pope has written extensively on the priesthood and the theology of love, chastity, and sexuality, none of this monumental work is even alluded to. . . . Avery Dulles' superb book *The Priestly Office* . . . De Lubac, Congar, Guardini, and von Balthasar are all missing." Groeschel, "Priests In Crisis," *Inside the Vatican*, November 2000: 60.

[12] Galot, *Theology of the Priesthood*, 222.

[13] George A. Aschenbrenner, SJ, *Quickening the Fire in Our Midst: The Challenge of Diocesan Priestly Spirituality* (Chicago: Loyola University Press, 2002), 16.

[14] Cozzens, *Changing Face*, 27.

[15] Groeschel, "Priests in Crisis," 61, emphasis in original.

[16] Aschenbrenner, *Quickening the Fire*, 22.

[17] Cardinal Joseph Ratzinger, *Behold the Pierced One* (San Francisco: Ignatius Press, 1986), 26.

[18] Raymond E. Brown, *Priest and Bishop* (London: Geoffrey Chapman, 1970), 26.

[19] Power, *A Spiritual Theology*, 52.

[20] Ibid., 52, 76.

[21] Thomas O'Meara, *The Theology of Ministry* (Ramsey: Paulist Press, 1983).

[22] From the catechetical instructions of Saint John Mary Vianney, priest, taken from the Office of Readings, August 4.

[23] As quoted in Dolan, *Priests for the Third Millennium*, 285–87.

[24] Power, *A Spiritual Theology*, 96.

[25] Ibid., 101.

[26] Sipe, *Celibacy*, 54–55, emphasis in original.

[27] Ratzinger, *Behold the Pierced One*, 15–18.

[28] Ibid., 18–19.

[29] Ibid., 22.

[30] Ibid., 24–25.

[31] As quoted in the *National Catholic Register* 78, no. 43 (October 27–November 2, 2002), 5.

[32] Balthasar, *Explorations IV*, 390.

[33] John Paul II, *Gift and Mystery*.

[34] Cardinal Paul-Pierre Philippe, *The Virgin Mary and the Priesthood* (New York: Alba House, 1993), 13, 18, 97.

[35] As quoted in the *National Catholic Register*, September 22–28, 3.

[36] Balthasar, *Explorations IV*, 374–75.

Bibliography

Acklin, Thomas, OSB. "Tomorrow's Priests." *The Priest* 54, no. 12 (December 1998).

Aardweg, Gerard J. M. van den. *The Battle for Normality: A Guide for Self-Therapy for Homosexuality.* San Francisco: Ignatius Press, 1997.

American Psychiatric Association, *Diagnostic and Statistical Manual of Mental Disorders.* 3rd ed. Washington, D.C.: APA, 1980.

Aschenbrenner, George A., SJ. *Quickening the Fire in Our Midst: The Challenge of Diocesan Priestly Spirituality.* Chicago: Loyola University Press, 2002.

Balthasar, Hans Urs von. "Priestly Existence." *Explorations in Theology, Vol. II: Spouse of the Word.* San Francisco: Ignatius Press, 1991.

———. *Explorations in Theology, Vol. IV: Spirit and Institution.* San Francisco: Ignatius Press, 1995.

Bergner, Mario. *Setting Love in Order: Hope and Healing for the Homosexual.* Grand Rapids: Baker Books, 1995.

Blommer, Stephen J. "Answers to Questions about Sexual Orientation and Homosexuality." In Laura Schlessinger, foreword to *Coming Out Straight: Understanding and Healing Homosexuality,* by Richard Cohen. Winchester: Oakhill Press, 2000.

Boyea, Earl. "Another Face of the Priesthood." *First Things,* no. 110 (February 2001).

Brown, Raymond E. *The Critical Meaning of the Bible.* New York: Paulist Press, 1981.

———. *Priest and Bishop.* London: Geoffrey Chapman, 1970.

Carnes, Patrick. *Don't Call It Love: Recovery from Sexual Addiction.* New York: Bantam, 1991.

———. *Out of the Shadows: Understanding Sexual Addiction.* Center City, MN: Hazelden Publishing, 1993.

———. *A Gentle Path through the Twelve Steps: The Classic Guide for All People in the Process of Recovery.* Center City, MN: Hazeldon, 1993.

Caulfield, Brian, "Homosexuals Who Change: Psychology's Dogma Breaking Down." *National Catholic Register* 78, no. 28 (July 14–20, 2002).

Clark, Keith. "Celibate Life Offers Insights." *Review for Religious* 59, no. 2 (March–April 2000).

Cochini, Christian, SJ. *The Apostolic Origins of Priestly Celibacy.* San Francisco: Ignatius Press, 1990.

Cohen, Richard. *Coming Out Straight: Understanding and Healing Homosexuality.* Winchester, VA: Oakhill Press, 2000.

Coleman, Gerald D., SS. *Homosexuality: Catholic Teaching and Pastoral Practice.* New York: Paulist Press, 1995.

———. *Human Sexuality: An All-Embracing Gift.* New York: Alba House, 1992.

Congregation for the Clergy. *Directory on the Ministry and Life of Priests.* Vatican City: Libreria Editrice Vaticana, 1994.

Coppens, J. "Old Testament Priesthood." *Priesthood and Celibacy.* Milan, 1972.

Cozzens, Donald B. *The Changing Face of the Priesthood: A Reflection on the Priest's Crisis of Soul.* Collegeville: Liturgical Press, 2000.

———. "Telling the Truth." *The Tablet,* May 8, 2000.

Dallas, Joe. *Desires in Conflict: Answering the Struggle for Sexual Identity.* Eugene, OR: Harvest House Publishers, 1991.

Dolan, Timothy M. *Priests for the Third Millennium.* Huntington, IN: Our Sunday Visitor, 2000.

Drummond, Thomas. "Fundamental Problem Underlying Sexual Abuse: A Broken Contract." Newsletter of the New

Life Institute for Human Development, vol. 10, no. 2 (Spring 2002).

Dulles, Avery, SJ. *The Priestly Office: A Theological Reflection.* Mahwah, NJ: Paulist Press, 1997.

Earle, Ralph and Gregory Crow. *Lonely All the Time: Recognizing, Understanding, and Overcoming Sex Addiction, for Addicts and Co-dependents.* Phoenix: Tri Star, 1998.

Elliott, Michelle. *Female Sexual Abuse of Children.* New York: Guilford Press, 1993.

Freud, Sigmund. *The Standard Edition of the Complete Psychological Works of Sigmund Freud.* 24 vols. Translated by James Strachey. London: Hogarth Press, 1955.

Galot, Jean, SJ. *Theology of the Priesthood.* San Francisco: Ignatius Press, 1985.

Gartner, Richard B. *Betrayal as Boys.* New York: Guilford Press, 1999.

Greeley, Andrew. "Bishops Paralyzed Over Heavily Gay Priesthood." *National Catholic Reporter,* November 10, 1989.

Groeschel, Benedict J., CFR. *From Scandal to Hope.* Huntington, IN: Our Sunday Visitor, 2002.

———. "Priests in Crisis." *Inside the Vatican,* November 2000.

———. *Stumbling Blocks or Stepping Stones?* Mahwah, NJ: Paulist Press, 1987.

Harvey, John F., OSFS. *The Truth about Homosexuality: The Cry of the Faithful.* San Francisco: Ignatius Press, 1996.

Heid, Stefan. *Celibacy in the Early Church: The Beginnings of a Discipline of Obligatory Continence for Clerics in East and West.* San Francisco: Ignatius Press, 2000.

Helminiak, Daniel A. *What the Bible Really Says about Homosexuality.* New Mexico: Alamo Press, 2000.

Horst, Elizabeth A. *Recovering the Lost Self: Shame-Healing for Victims of Clergy Sexual Abuse.* Collegeville: Liturgical Press, 1998.

Jenkins, Philip. "The Myth of the Pedophile Priest." *Pittsburgh Post-Gazette,* March 3, 2002.

————. *Pedophiles and Priests: Anatomy of a Contemporary Crisis.*
New York: Oxford University Press, 2001.

Johnson, Luke Timothy. "A Disembodied 'Theology of the
Body': John Paul II on Love, Sex, and Pleasure."
Commonweal, vol. cxxviii, no. 2 (January 26, 2001).

Kohut, Heinz. *The Analysis of the Self.* New York: International
Universities Press, 1971.

Lawler, Philip. "Whose Responsibility." *Catholic World Report*
12, no. 7 (July 2002).

Legrand, H. M. "The Presidency of the Eucharist according to
the Ancient Tradition." *Worship* 53 (1979).

Lewes, Kenneth. *Psychoanalysis and Male Homosexuality.* London:
Jason Aronson, 1995.

Marzheuser, Richard, "A New Generation Is on the Rise in
Seminaries," *Seminary Journal,* Fall 1999.

Masters, William, Virginia E. Johnson, and Robert C. Kolodny.
Masters and Johnson on Sex and Human Loving. Boston: Little
Brown & Company, 1988.

McGovern, Thomas. *Priestly Celibacy Today.* Princeton, NJ:
Scepter Publishers, 1998.

Michael, Robert T., John H. Gagnon, Edward O. Laumann, and
Gina Kolate. *Sex in America: A Definitive Survey.* Boston:
Warner Books, 1994.

Moberly, Elizabeth R. *Homosexuality: A New Christian Ethic.*
Cambridge: James Clarke & Co., 1983.

National Conference of Catholic Bishops. *Priests for a New
Millennium: A Series of Essays on the Ministerial Priesthood.*
Washington, D.C.: Secretariat for Priestly Life and Ministry
United States Conference of Catholic Bishops, 2000.

Nicolosi, Joseph. *Reparative Therapy of Male Homosexuality: A
New Clinical Approach.* Northvale: Jason Aronson, 1997.

O'Brien, John J., CP. "Intimacy." *The New Dictionary of Catholic
Spirituality.* Edited by Michael Downey. Collegeville:
Liturgical Press, 1993.

O'Connor, Noreen and Loanna Ryan. *Lesbianism and Psychoanalysis: Wild Desires and Mistaken Identities.* New York: Columbia University Press, 1993.

O'Keefe, Mark, OSB. *In Persona Christi: Reflections on Priestly Identity and Holiness.* St. Meinrad, IN: Abbey Press, 1998.

———. *The Ordination of a Priest: Reflections on the Priesthood in the Rite of Ordination.* St. Meinrad, IN: Abbey Press, 1999.

Payne, Leanne. *Crisis in Masculinity.* Grand Rapids: Baker Books, 1985.

Philibert, Paul, OP. "Issues for a Theology of Priesthood: A Status Report." Chapter 1 in *The Theology of the Priesthood.* Edited by Donald J. Goergen, Ann Garrido, and Benedict M. Ashley. Collegeville: Liturgical Press, 2000.

Philippe, Paul-Pierre, OP. *The Virgin Mary and the Priesthood.* New York: Alba House, 1993.

Pope John Paul II. *Gift and Mystery: On the Fiftieth Anniversary of My Priestly Ordination.* New York: Doubleday, 1996.

Pope John Paul II. *The Theology of the Body: Human Love in the Divine Plan.* Boston: Pauline Books & Media, 1997.

Power, Dermot. *A Spiritual Theology of the Priesthood: The Mystery of Christ and the Mission of the Priest.* Washington, D.C.: Catholic University of America Press, 1998.

Ratzinger, Joseph. *Behold the Pierced One.* San Francisco: Ignatius Press, 1986.

Reinishch, June M. *The Kinsey Institute New Report on Sex.* New York: St. Martin's Press, 1990.

Reisman, Judith A., Edward W. Eichel, John H. Court, and J. Gordon Muir, eds. *Kinsey, Sex, and Fraud: The Indoctrination of a People.* Lafayette: Huntington House, 1990.

Rose, Michael S. *Goodbye, Good Men.* Washington: Regency Press, 2002.

Rossetti, Stephen J. "The Catholic Church and Child Sexual Abuse." *America* 186, no. 13 (April 22, 2002).

———. *A Tragic Grace: The Catholic Church and Child Sexual Abuse.* Collegeville: Liturgical Press, 1996.

Schillebeeckx, Edward. *Ministry: Leadership in the Community of Jesus Christ.* New York: Crossroad, 1981.

Schoenherr, Richard and Larry Young. *Full Pews and Empty Altars: Demographics of the Priest Shortage in United States Catholic Dioceses.* University of Wisconsin Press, 1993.

Scroggs, Robin. *The New Testament and Homosexuality.* Philadelphia: Fortress Press, 1983.

Shaughnessy, Paul. "The Gay Priest Problem." *Catholic World Report* 10, no. 10 (November 2000).

Sipe, A. W. Richard. *Celibacy: A Way of Loving, Living, and Serving.* Ligouri, MO: Triumph Books, 1996.

Stickler, A. M. "The Evolution of the Discipline of Celibacy in the Western Church from the End of the Patristic Era to the Council of Trent." In J. Coppens, ed. *Priesthood and Celibacy.* Milan, 1972.

Weigel, George, "Church Must Become More Catholic Not Less," *Pittsburgh Catholic,* May 17, 2002. Originally appeared in *The Los Angeles Times,* May 5, 2002.

———. *The Courage to Be Catholic: Crisis, Reform, and the Future of the Church.* New York: Basic Books, 2002.

———. *Witness to Hope: The Biography of Pope John Paul II.* New York: Harper Collins, 1999.

Wicai, Hillary. "Clergy by the Numbers." *Congregations* 27, no. 2 (March/April 2001).

The Great Life

Essays on Doctrine and Holiness

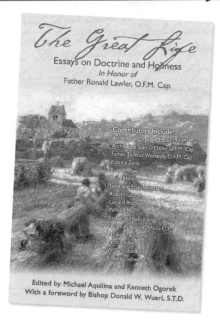

The Great Life

Essays on Doctrine and Holiness
In Honor of
Father Ronald Lawler, O.F.M. Cap.

Contributors Include:
Archbishop Charles Chaput O.F.M. Cap.
Archbishop Seán O'Malley O.F.M. Cap.
Father Thomas Weinandy O.F.M. Cap.
Katrina Zeno
Russell Shaw
Scott Hahn
Janet and Brian Benestad
Robert George
Gerard Bradley
William May
Evelyn and John Billings
Father Augustine DiNoia O.P.
Father Kris Stubna
Patrick Riley
William Saunders
Robert Lockwood

Edited by Michael Aquilina and Kenneth Ogorek
With a foreword by Bishop Donald W. Wuerl, S.T.D.

F ather Ronald Lawler, O.F.M. Cap. (1926-2003), was a priest, teacher, author, theologian, catechist, spiritual advisor, and mentor, who lived the great life of faith and encouraged others to join him in loving Christ and His Church. In *The Great Life*, those who knew and loved Father Lawler honor him by continuing his work. This collection of essays is not only an invitation to know the Faith, but also to love, live, and teach it from the heart of the Church.

> **❝** The good influence that Father Ronald had on so many Capuchins and diocesan priests cannot be exaggerated. **❞**
>
> —*Archbishop Seán P. O'Malley*

EMMAUS
ROAD
PUBLISHING

(800) 398-5470 / www.emmausroad.org